THE Kid BOOK

Surprising Truths About People We Call Kids

Vicki L. Barnes

The Kid Book
Surprising Truths About People We Call Kids
by Vicki L. Barnes

Copyright © 1999 by Vicki L. Barnes
All rights reserved

Published by
For Kids Only, Inc.
Newport Beach, California

Book production by Ad Graphics, Tulsa, Oklahoma

Illustrations by Jean Suddaith

Printed in the United States of America
ISBN: 1-929568-05-3

iv

DEDICATION

To my parents Jack and Fran Threlkeld, better known as Honey and Poppa, who consistently show their children, grandchildren, and great grandchildren how to live life with character, unselfishness, and joy. As owners of the "hang-out house," they have influenced the lives of many kids with their unfailing acceptance and unconditional love. Because they took the time to accept us for who we were, they gave us the confidence we needed to succeed.

ACKNOWLEDGMENTS

Thanks to the encouragement and support of so many wonderful people in my life this book has come to fruition. My husband, Fred, who was my unofficial editor, main encourager and sounding board. My boys, Matt and Tyler, who let me parent them without understanding their personality types. Amy and her four boys, who represent the four personality types, were a great source for stories and examples.

Unwavering Armene Humber who walked beside me every step of the way. She did it all, from consulting, to writing my bio and book description, to introducing me to her brother Frank A. Haas who contributed the subtitle and tons of creative advice.

Courageous Suzzi Marquis who edited the book before the editor. She said, "Vicki never met a comma she didn't like."

Flexible Jim Weems at Ad Graphics who named the book and endured my endless bouts of "mind changing."

Creative Carl Spady who read my mind for cover ideas.

Generous Jean Suddaith who gave me the gift of her talent to design the personality kids between the chapters.

Talented Susan Titus Osborn, my official editor, who is patient, encouraging, and good at her job.

Supportive Jim and Johanna Townsend who have become dream makers in several ways.

Thank you to my writers group, who for the last seven years have been saying, "Put your message in writing." My Focus group who gave "Tough Love" at all the right times.

To the many people who have supported me in prayer and reminded me that ALL things are possible through God who gives us strength, I thank you.

TABLE OF CONTENTS

Introduction xi

SECTION ONE

The Adults
Learning about Yourselves First 1

Chapter 1
The Promoters 11

Chapter 2
The Planners 22

Chapter 3
The Producers 36

Chapter 4
The Peacekeepers 46

SECTION TWO

The KIDS 59

Chapter 5
Perky Promoters 65

Chapter 6
Precise Planners 77

Chapter 7
Powerful Producers 87

Chapter 8
Patient Peacekeepers 97

SECTION THREE

More or Less Alike? 107

Chapter 9
Similarities and Differences 111

Chapter 10
Understanding US 121

SECTION FOUR

Using What You've Learned 137

Chapter 11
The Parenting Kit 140

Chapter 12
Doctor Foster's Lessons 148

Chapter 13
Speaking Out for the Kids 163

Thank You Notes
from the KIDS 175

INTRODUCTION

During my first year of teaching, the children in my fourth grade class showed me the importance personality types play in understanding and relating more effectively with others. I soon learned that I could group my students into different personality types, and in time, I realized that each personality had different wants and needs. A serious young student named David taught me an important lesson regarding the different personality types.

The large chart of our daily schedule on my classroom wall showed that at 10:30 a.m. math would begin. However, at 10:30 a.m. the second week of school I said, "Girls and boys, it's a beautiful day, let's go outside and have a science lesson."

With that announcement nine-year-old David burst into tears. I walked to his desk and asked, "David, what is the matter?" With tears streaming down his face he said, "The daily schedule says that math will be at 10:30 a.m. We have not had math at 10:30 a.m. once this year."

Truthfully, I didn't know if David was correct or not. I hadn't noticed because I'm a spontaneous, flexible person who doesn't give much attention to schedules. Structure isn't important to me, but it certainly was to David.

In an attempt to save David from being teased for crying, I said, "David, you are right, the schedule does say math at 10:30 a.m. Let's take a vote. How many want to do math at 10:30 a.m. and science at 1:30 p.m. like the schedule states?"

In my head I was thinking that perhaps three or four kids would raise their hands. David would feel supported, and I'd go on winging it the rest of the year. About 75 percent of my class raised their hands. This statistic I later learned was representative of the percentage of the population who like some degree of structure.

Up to this point, it had never occurred to me that there was any other way to do things besides loose and casual. I tried very hard that first year not to be my usual "wing it—fly by the seat of my pants" self. My class wanted a schedule and structure. I wanted to meet their needs, so I was as organized as I could be for a "go with the flow" personality type.

Did this flash of insight into the differences in personalities start me down the path that has culminated into this book? I honestly would have to admit that I forgot to apply what my class had taught me when I arrived at the next stop on my life schedule—parenting. I raised my children without the advantage of understanding the concept of personality types. I failed to fully understand my children and meet some of their needs because I did not relate to them according to their personality types. Instead I just assumed they would want to do, think, and be like me. I was wrong.

Now that my sons are grown and on their own, I know a great deal about personality types and the needs of each type. I keep wishing there were such things as "Do-Over Coupons." I would redeem mine to use what I have learned.

The first thing I would do over is to follow the biblical principle that states: Train up children in the way they should go—the way God intended them to be. To me this meant to figure out each child's personality and raise him or her according to what's best for that personality type. I am writing this book because the people in my audiences know that there are no "Do-Over Coupons." They want to understand the kids in their lives and get it right the first time. They have requested, over and over for me to write down what I say in my seminars on personality types.

One attendee named Amy, the mother of four, was finally the one who motivated me to start. She said, "Sitting here today listening to you, I know I'm totally doing it wrong with my second child because he is the most unlike me. My oldest and I have very similar personalities. I do fine with him, most of the time. My third child is a slow-paced, gentle, sweet soul, and I just don't understand her. My fourth is even more powerful than I am. I'm going to need to know everything I can if either of us is going to survive. Please help me to understand more about my children." Then she paused, took a breath, and said, "But don't write your book for the adults, write your message for the sake of the children."

Suddenly, I realized she was right. From my early elementary teaching days to today, I have been an advocate for children. I went home and started this book that same day. Faces of children whose parents don't understand their personality types kept me company as I wrote. In my seminars I see and hear adults who are clueless about the personality types of their children.

Many of the situations of not understanding a child's personality seem to fall into defined categories. One of the largest categories is the rigid, intense, and demanding adult with the naturally good, self-motivated child. I wince inwardly as I watch this great child shrink from unfair pressure instead of blooming as he or she could if a little encouragement had been applied.

A perfect example of this situation is in the movie *October Sky*. The child hero finally bloomed, but he had to overcome paralyzing pressure from his father. Rent the movie. Watch it with your children. Be courageous enough to ask your children if you ever treated them the way the father in this movie treated his son. Be ready to *listen* and just take in what your children say. If you don't like what you hear, keep it to yourself. Listen with your eyes. Watch their body language. What are they afraid to say? Sometimes what they don't say speaks louder than what they do say. This is not the time to argue or defend yourself. Say, "Thank you for your input. I will think about this. Later could we talk about this some more?"

Finish this book and then meet with your family. Tell them what you've learned about yourself and what you've learned about them. Apologize if necessary and tell them you love them and really want to understand them and will work on doing that. For you who like to be in control, you will not lose control over your children. You will gain their respect and love.

Another category of misunderstanding personality types is in establishing boundaries. Knowing which child needs strong boundaries with clear, fair rules is important. Equally important is knowing which child does not need to be raised with such a tight grip. Those whose personality types are prone to rebel against boundaries are exactly the ones who need structure and boundaries most. Here I see parents who aren't consistent, structured, or intentional enough to enforce the rules and logical consequences. Yet, these must be in place for this child to learn self-control and discipline.

Jordan was the child I pictured for this situation. He was born a free spirit. His non-conforming nature got him in trouble from day one. Was he a bad kid? No, he was just the product of his personality and a family system that did not have the right boundaries in place. Being a good kid at heart he became discouraged with this self-defeating behavior. His behavior was crying out for guidance. Jordan's parents finally cared enough about him to invest their time in "Tough Love" classes. The concepts, disciplines, and boundaries of Tough Love helped Jordan and his parents survive his teenage years.

Another category of parent-child personality mismanagement is the logical, often unemotional adult with the gentle tender-hearted child. Watching this adult try to turn an emotionally based child into a logical, calculating analyzer is heartbreaking. To see this played out go to any soccer or Little League baseball game. There you will usually find one tough, strong-willed, competitive adult pushing a non-competitive, easygoing, gentle child to develop the killer instinct. It's not going to happen. The only thing that is going to be killed in this situation is the child's spirit.

My favorite justice story is of a powerful attorney in our area who was determined his child would excel at swimming the way he had. His child, a tender heart, didn't have Daddy's drive, tenacity, or competitive spirit. One day his son's team was competing against my son's team. There was Dad in his suit and tie racing back and forth the length of the pool screaming directions at his son as he raced. This scene repeated itself for several races. As his son lost each race I watched the child's body language become more and more discouraged and desperate. Suddenly on the last lap of his son's race the child shot out in the lead. The father jumped up in the air with excitement, lost his balance, and crashed into the pool on top of another swimmer. His son won the race. The race was declared a forfeit due to outside interference. It was the first time all day I saw the child smile.

I love kids. They are the best gifts in life. It's going to be hard to be a child in the 21st century. Parents, grandparents, caregivers, teachers, coaches, troop leaders, and other relatives have a huge impact on children's lives. These adults need to know as much about each child's personality as possible. Imagine what a painful year David would have had if I continued to ignore schedules, rules, and deadlines in my classroom. I, however, was the adult, and it was up to me to observe, learn, and change when necessary.

I am writing this book as a spokesperson for children. The purpose of this book is to aid adults in raising children in the way God intended them to be. When we train them with an understanding of who they are, we will help develop them into who they were meant to be.

Most adults want to understand and meet the personality needs of children. They just don't understand or speak the language of personality types. After reading this book a person will be able to understand and speak the language of the four personality types. We are always going to speak our own personality language the most fluently. We will understand and identify with the people with our same personality type the most. But let's learn three other new personality languages.

Even if you struggle, try speaking the language of the personality type of the child with whom you are working. I have a file full of correspondence from adults who shared success stories about finally understanding the child with whom they were struggling. When you speak the language of someone's personality type, that individual hears the language of understanding and love.

SECTION ONE

The Adults

Learning about Yourselves First

SECTION ONE

The Adults

Learning about Yourselves First

A favorite speaker of mine, Tony Alessandro, often talks about the Platinum Rule. He defines it as, "Treat others the way they want to be treated." But before treating others the way they want to be treated we have to look at ourselves. How should you be treating yourself? Do you know? I find many people in my audiences know more about their computers than they do about themselves.

The goal here is to raise children the way they were intended— but first we have to look at the people doing the raising. We have to know about adult personality types before we can take on the kids. So, let's start with you.

In this first section you will find out your core personality type, which includes the good news and the bad news. You will learn more than you thought possible about yourself. In the next section, we will explore the kids and who they are. Then we will work on the teaching part in the last sections of this book.

The "You" Part

Take the Personality Type Assessment on the following pages and follow the scoring directions.

Personality Type Assessment

In the 10 sets of words or word groups below, you will choose those that *accurately* describe you—not how you would like to be! **MOVING ACROSS** the page, from left to right, rate each set of words, placing your rating number in the gray shaded area in front of each word set. Use the rating system below. When you have filled in all the lines **ACROSS**, **ADD DOWN** each of the columns 1 through 10 to learn your core personality type.

Rate each set of word groups by thinking about which fits you. *Use each number once only per line.* Give the following ratings in the gray areas in front of the column: **4**=most often or best   **3**= sometimes   **2**= hardly ever   **1**=least

EXAMPLE

A description of me:	3 Social	1 Practical	4 Decisive	2 Fair
1. A description of me:	Cheerful	Purposeful	Forceful	Tactful
2. This group of words best describes me:	Active, enthusiastic, high-spirited, fun	Serious, intense, honest, plans ahead, wants things right	Decisive, makes things happen, leader	Kind, patient, supportive, easy-going
3. I like:	Activities and variety	Structure and order	To be right	Steadiness and balance
4. I am motivated by:	Fun and freedom	Belonging and contributing	Power and results	Peace and harmony
5. When working with a group I:	Want to be with a fun group, that doesn't take everything so seriously but gets the work done	Get frustrated with those who make mistakes and are not conscientious	Want to take responsibility for seeing that the group gets it done	Want to be in a group where there's compatibility and cooperation.
6. A concern is:	Boring repetition and same old routines	Making mistakes and unpredictability	Incompetent people and inefficiency	Rushed schedules and work piling up

	Loss of relationships	Change and disorder	Loss of control	Loss of harmony
7. I fear:				
8. I need:	Recognition and affirmations	To be appreciated for my quality work	Respect for my accomplishments	Acceptance for who I am not what I do
9. Under stress I can become:	Fragmented and disorganized	Moody and withdrawn	Dictatorial and assertive	Overwhelmed and exhausted
11. Areas I need to work on:	Interrupting	Being critical	Being impatient	Being indecisive
12. The group of words that best describe my strengths:	Inventive Intuitive Optimistic Energetic Encouraging	Dependable Thoughtful Organized Integrity Honest	Leadership Achievement Perseverance Visionary Drive	Diplomatic Compassionate Contented Clarity Kind
13. I can be:	Persuasive	Diligent	Competitive	Accommodating
14. People who know me might use this description:	Charismatic, full of ideas, with lots going on	Dependable, organized, practical, does things perfectly	Self directed, in charge, determined and accomplishes a great deal	Diplomatic, peacemaker, kindhearted, balanced and a good listener
Add down each column for the TOTAL. Please start on the next page to understand your core personality type.	TOTAL____	TOTAL____	TOTAL____	TOTAL____

Now that you have a score at the bottom of each of the four columns, look for your highest score.

For each column there will a group name, a group color, and a group symbol. Each of us is unique; yet, each of us has a group of core traits that are very similar to traits others have. It's these similarities we will focus on.

Why a group name? Names are a way to identify, distinguish, and signify the uniqueness and specialness about us. Each name will describe and identify the personality type as a group.

Why colors? Using colors with their various shades and hues help us to see the similarities and the differences. Our commonality is one group color, and our individuality is all the shades and hues of that color.

Why symbols? People learn and grasp concepts in different ways. Using symbols is a visual way to present the concept of each personality type.

So if your highest score is in Column One, your personality name is Promoter. Your group color is Yellow, and your group symbol is a Spring.

Why Promoter? The common traits in this group involve the sociability of people. People in this group are relationship-oriented, people-persons, who love to encourage, recruit, and network. Promoting people, relationships, fun, and the good life is their mission.

Why Yellow for the Promoters? Yellow is the color of the sun and stars, bright and sparkling. This personality type has charisma and tends to sparkle. Yellow is an attention-getting color, and this group likes attention. Yellow is the color of big, bright, bold sunflowers, and the personality type can be big, bright, and bold.

Why Springs? Springs are flexible, malleable, and can accommodate a great deal of movement and stress. This personality group represents flexibility, animation, and resiliency. They take many of the stresses of life in stride.

If you got your highest score in Column Two, your personality name is Planner. Your color is Blue, and your symbol is a Box.

Why Planner? The people represented in this group are practical, analytical, problem solvers. They are continually looking for the best way to do something. They plan life and then live it!

Why Blue? Bodies of water appear blue and are often deep, covering large areas. The people in this group are deep personality types and represent a large percentage of the population. Blue is an expression that has come to mean sad or moody. This group experiences more of these feelings than other personality groups.

Why a Box? Planners are people who like to have a place for everything and everything in its place. So a box provides that place. Also this group likes boundaries, rules, and guidelines, and a box represents these traits.

If you got your highest score in Column Three, your name is Producer. Your color is Red, and your symbol is the Check Mark.

Why Producer? This group lives to achieve and accomplish. "Time is money" and "Make it happen" are two of their favorite life mottoes. This group finds fulfillment in human accomplishments. These are our human "doings." Do, do, do, achieve, achieve, accomplish, accomplish, are the words of the internal voices playing in the heads of most producers.

Why Red? Studies show that red worn in competitive sports is an intimidating color to an opponent. People in this group are usually competitive and can be intimidating.

Why the Check Mark? Producers like to get it done, check it off the list, and move on to bigger and better achievements. The check symbolizes completion and accomplishment, and that's what Producers are definitely about.

If you got your highest score in Column Four, your name is Peacekeeper. Your color is Green, and your symbol is an Oval.

Why Peacekeeper? The personality types in this group have characteristics and attributes that make them natural diplomats and mediators. They are kind, balanced people who have a strong sense of fair play and acceptance. This group wants "peace at any price." Peacekeepers do not like to "make waves" or "rock the boat" of life.

Why Green? As we observe nature there are many shades of green. The trees and foliage of nature are a feast for the eyes. This green part of nature has a soothing and calming effect on the observer. Most Peacekeepers are a source of calm and harmony in their environments.

Why an Oval? An oval has no sharp edges or rough sides, so it just rolls along. It is also the shape of an egg. Peacekeepers are known as "good eggs," because they don't get their feathers ruffled easily.

In the next four chapters of this section I discuss in depth the four personality types from the adult perspective. Start with the personality type that was your highest score, then second highest, third, and then lowest. Depending on your scores you many find yourself identifying with both of your two top scores. If you have even or balanced scores, start with the Peacekeeper chapter and see if this is the most like you. If not, read the chapter of your next highest score. Read all the chapters until you find the one that best captures your traits.

Before you start to read, please study the chart on the next page. I use tee shirts to represent the personality types. The graphic design on each shirt is yet another tool to help you identify your core personality type. As you complete this book be thinking about personality type tee shirts. What is the one you wear most of the time? We all have a core personality type and a representative tee shirt for that type. After you pick the shirt, think about the shade of the color.

I am a Promoter, and my shade would be bright yellow like a taxicab. The Promoter shirt represents my core. Of the four tee shirts, yellow is the one I wear most.

I use the tee shirt concept to show that we need to wear the tee shirts of other personalities at times. As a mother I need to put the green Peacekeeper shirt over the top of my core yellow Promoter shirt. As a person who works with teams in organizations, I often need to wear the red Producer shirt to get the results the clients want. I rarely wear the blue Planner shirt because my husband never leaves home without his.

This book teaches you to know your personality core and to know the personality core of the children in your life. Then, you can figure out what is the right tee shirt to wear to meet the needs of each child. As we travel though life, we need all four tee shirts in our backpack. You never know when you will need to put another personality type shirt over your core shirt so you can understand, relate, and speak the language of another personality type.

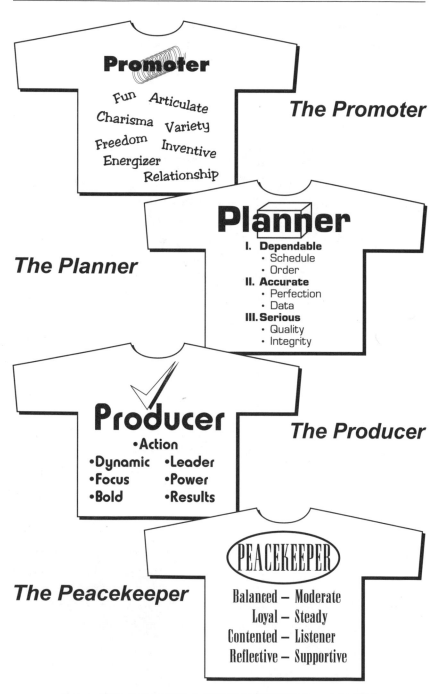

The Promoter

Promoter
Fun Articulate
Charisma Variety
Freedom Inventive
Energizer
Relationship

The Planner

Planner
I. **Dependable**
 • Schedule
 • Order
II. **Accurate**
 • Perfection
 • Data
III. **Serious**
 • Quality
 • Integrity

The Producer

Producer
•Action
•Dynamic •Leader
•Focus •Power
•Bold •Results

The Peacekeeper

PEACEKEEPER
Balanced – Moderate
Loyal – Steady
Contented – Listener
Reflective – Supportive

People Skills Series VICKI BARNES SEMINARS Copyright 1985

10

CHAPTER 1

The Promoters

Promoter • Yellow • Spring

Personality Characteristics

Promoters are charismatic people who are able to recruit and enlist the help of others. Their enthusiasm is contagious, and they are Pied Pipers by nature. Getting people to join in is one of their specialties. Promoters are people persons who use personal charm and strong social skills to influence their world. These spirited people are adept at fitting in with those around them. Socially sensitive Promoters prefer to be around others. Youthful in manner, joking, and playful, this yellow group often has wild personal stories to tell. Articulate and entertaining, they enjoy an audience and the spotlight. With a positive focus and a natural liveliness, they generate energy, excitement, and motivation in others.

Promoters are very intuitive people. They know because they know. Don't ask them how they know because they will just say it's a "gut hunch." This personality type has a sixth sense about them. They read people well. Most are good at understanding body language and non-verbal communication.

Recently we were at a dinner party. On the way home I told my husband that one of our favorite young couples were finally pregnant after years of attempting to become pregnant. He said, "Where was I when they made the announcement?"

"Oh, they didn't announce it yet," I explained.

He then gave me the I-want-to-argue-with-you look. But he knew our history proves I've been right too many times to argue. "So would you mind telling what you saw that I missed," he requested.

"It's the new way Scott watched Kim that tipped me off. He was suddenly her personal bodyguard. She was suddenly breakable, and if he watched her every minute then she wouldn't break."

A month later we received a phone call from Scott and Kim announcing their pregnancy. My husband hung up and said, "Can I learn the intuitive thing from you?"

It is no accident that Promoters are relationship oriented. This yellow group makes their decisions with their hearts. The first filter for a decision is how will this affect people's values and needs. Putting people first is a natural for this encouraging, social, heart-filled type.

Promoters are adept at building alliances and using relationships to accomplish work. My Promoter friend Todd bought a fixer upper house. All his friends thought he'd never follow through and get his house finished. Todd said, "Oh, just watch. It will be finished sooner than you think." Todd used the Huckleberry Finn/ Tom Sawyer method. He had work parties and made them so much fun a person didn't want to miss any. It seemed everyone worked hard on the house, except Todd. He raced around keeping everyone in food and drink, while popping hysterical jokes. Todd's friends finished his house in record time.

Spontaneity, fast-paced, and decisive action are qualities of this yellow group. Starting projects and events are their specialty. They also enjoy the finish—especially if there is a celebration. But they often get bogged down in the middle. Because they love life to be action-packed, they live in fear of dull moments, boring people, and slow-paced anything. Being on the cutting edge of events, happenings, and trends is essential to them. These spontaneous, high-energy people are quick-paced and animated. Life must be an exciting adventure filled with inspiration, unlimited possibilities, and fun people.

When Promoters are bored or stressed their verbal behavior intensifies, and they may tend to exaggerate for effect in their stories, talk too much, or interrupt. They become fragmented, ambivalent, and disorganized.

-Needs

Relationships

Promoters truly love people, so it should be expected that relationships are given a high priority in their lives. Because they have smiles on their faces and find conversation easy, they have the uncanny ability to put almost anyone at ease. Promoters are great storytellers and can hold the attention of an audience, be it large or small.

They are encouragers par excellence from motivating the disheartened to intuitively coming along side to support people and their aspirations. Promoters are the cheerleaders of life.

Most have good people skills. Their quick wit, charisma, command of language, and ability to laugh at themselves are traits that enhance both their personal and business relationships. Skilled as relationship builders, these are people who care. People seem to sense that Promoters provide a safe place to share their hearts.

I sometimes travel with another Promoter speaker named Stephanie. Her shade of yellow is the brightest there is. She can have someone tell her a life story in an airport bathroom while she washes her hands and puts on lipstick. On the plane she makes two new friends before take off and three more during the flight.

When I travel with Stephanie I wear my Planner shirt. I become the serious one. Often I sleep on planes. While I sleep these people tell her incredible secrets about their lives. On the drive from the airport to home she shares their stories with me. I always say, "You learned all those stories on a two-hour flight. I can't imagine what would happen on a Trans-Atlantic flight."

Popularity

The yellow group enjoys liking, but they also have a high need to be liked. Popularity generally comes to them partly because of their cheerful dispositions and caring attitudes. This yellow group knows the power of the concept: *So, There You Are* — Here I am. Finding out what others need and seeing they get it adds to their popularity.

Their self-effacing humor and willingness to "tell all" about their lives and "hear all" about yours makes them easy to be around. Promoters know no strangers. Making friends quickly is easy for them. Many have "New Best Friend Syndrome."

Being a bright, taxi cab yellow Promoter, I collect friends in supermarket lines and restaurant bathrooms. Anyone I'm with for over five minutes has the potential of becoming my "New Best Friend." For our fifth anniversary my husband gave us a weekend at a time management seminar. He didn't need it, but he knew if he didn't go with me I'd skip the seminar and go shopping. During the training it became abundantly clear that managing all the plethora of friendships in my life was consuming most of my time. At the end of the weekend we had to summarize and share our action steps. I had one—go home and dump my best friends. The audience gave a collective gasp. My husband said in his nonchalant style, "Don't worry. She has three hundred and sixty-five, one for every day of the year. She'll make new ones."

Recognition

Promoters need recognition for their accomplishments. They thrive on positive affirmations and like to see facial expressions and body language that express approval. Don't be stingy with words of appreciation, as it is extremely discouraging for a Promoter to be deprived of positive feedback. For most of this group, encouraging words are food for the soul.

They spend much of their time pumping others up. They really do need to see the inflation process happening and receive feedback that they have made a difference. Promoters will hang in with you and your problems as long as you affirm them and show some progress toward getting it together and working toward living victoriously. Without progress and feedback, color them gone.

Being the eternal optimists, Promoters are cheerleaders of life. They believe victorious living is theirs, if they only think they can. Attitude is everything. This yellow group particularly dislikes criticism for themselves and others. Often they respond to criticism with verbal attacks.

Variety

Repetition and details have a tough time holding the interest of a Promoter. They need things to be fresh, new, and exciting. Starts are a specialty, and because their enthusiasm spills over onto others, many jump on the bandwagon with them. However, once the newness and initial excitement wears off and repetition starts to set in, Promoters tend to lose interest. Finishes and follow through may be difficult for that reason.

Multi-tasking is easy and enjoyable for this group. They like to juggle a lot of balls at a time. It is the thrill of the hunt. Can they make it? Risk and a sense of adventure are important.

Flexibility

Their openness to new ideas makes them ready to spring into action at a moment's notice. Promoters like to keep their options open. They are spontaneous and almost never have a problem changing plans mid-stream. They are not restricted by time constraints and are often poor time managers. Promoters struggle with being on time and having all the supplies needed to complete the task. This flexible group tends to misplace things. Don't give them the original of anything. They don't want that much responsibility.

Even though they are creative themselves, they do not find it difficult to get charged up about an idea that was not their own. They will even promote the idea and, like the Pied Pipers they are, will have people lined up behind them. These charismatic leaders attracts followers.

Attention

Whoever said, "All of life is a stage," must have been a Promoter. This yellow group always has a story to tell and the more listeners the better. I had a client who was in the professional placement industry. The company had inside sales people doing cold calling for job openings and outside sales people calling on companies to help them fill their employee needs. One of the outside sales people was Marty, a bright yellow Promoter.

Marty came flying into the office every few days usually around 2:30 p.m. or 3:00 p.m. She always had a story to tell. There was the story about looking for her car for three hours in the wrong parking structure. Finally she made friends with the security guard who drove her to the right parking structure. Then there was the afternoon she whirled in with this story. While having lunch with one of the vice presidents of her largest account the client choked on a sandwich and she preformed the Hiemlich Maneuver to save the client.

The minute Marty started to tell one of her stories everyone stopped dialing and listened to the latest adventure in "Marty's Mini-series." My client, the president of the company, was extremely frustrated with these interruptions. Marty, however, was his best salesperson, and he didn't want to upset her. I observed this event for a couple of weeks. I noticed that 2:30 to 3:00 o'clock was the low production point for the inside sales people. More milling around and trips to the coffee machines occurred then than any other time during the day. The days when Marty came in the production stopped for ten to fifteen minutes. After she left everyone had talked, socialized a short time, and been energized by Marty and her story. The hour after Marty was in the office was the most productive time all week. What time the company lost while Marty was on center stage was regained and exceeded after Marty left. Promoters are energizing storytellers.

Motives

Motives are the things that drive us. Having fun, particularly fun that is relationship- oriented, motivates Promoters. If you listen to this yellow group, you will hear the word *fun* used frequently. Jobs, relationships, or anything in which they are involved must be fun. Life must be fun.

This group can always find an excuse to have a party. They love giving surprise parties—often for people who don't like change, unpredictable circumstances, or surprises.

In the workplace, birthdays, engagements, marriages, or babies are always an excuse for Promoters to suggest an event. Promoters are great at getting the ball rolling for the party idea. Often they bog down in the details of the planning and following through.

As a young bride I loved having friends over. One Saturday we were having three couples over to celebrate one of the couple's anniversary. I got so busy decorating the house and table, planning the music, and devising a silly game, I forgot to plan the food. When the guests arrived I was at the market racing down the aisles throwing instant anything into my cart. The meal was a little unusual, but the conversation was lively, and everyone had a great time. If you want fine dining, go to a restaurant. If you want fun and the unexpected, go to a Promoter's house for dinner.

Good News – Bad News

First the good news. This group is casual and fun. They love having a great time in life and taking others along. They do not "sweat the small stuff," and "close enough" is good enough. People will follow them anywhere. And anywhere is often where they are going. Maps, plans, and directions are filled with too many boring details. This group likes to "wing it" and "shoot from the hip." "Leap and the net will appear" is one motto for these eternal optimists.

Promoters can really get themselves and often others into major messes. But the "God is Good Scenario" often seems to cover this casual style. God knows that Promoters are impulsive and don't always plan ahead, so He made them creative, innovative, inducing, inspirational, winsome, and energetic. These attributes get them out of their messes. No matter how disastrous their current mess is they get through it with the motivating thought of what a great story this is going to make!

The Lucille Ball Show, *I Love Lucy,* was a pure portrayal of a Promoting Yellow Spring. The entire series was based on Lucy's messes and how she extricated herself with the help of dear Ethel who was a Peacekeeper. Lucy's vivid imagination, desire for adventure, and little attention to details formed the foundation for the show.

This yellow group is innovative. They are the possibility people with an idea a minute. They are great brainstormers, but sometimes a little impractical. Often they can't implement their ideas. Many are forgetful and, if they don't write down their inspiration, they will forget. Others are so disorganized that even if they write it down they can't find it. Thus, a great concept dies.

Being caring supporters of people, they are generous and willing to share solutions and materials. Many a Promoter has said, "Oh, I have just the book for you." The problem is they don't follow through, and you don't get the promised help.

What do you think other personality types say about Promoters? The good news is they are fun, funny, tell great stories, usually know a joke or two, and are very friendly and upbeat. They are enjoyable to hang out with because they know how to turn a dull moment into a good time. They have lots of friends, and life around them is exciting, eventful, and energetic.

The bad news is they can be attention grabbing, obnoxious, interrupting, and conversation dominators. People who work with them talk about their lack of time management skills, flakiness, and undependability. Others say that they are often scattered and impulsive. They can get you into some real messes with their lack of attention to details.

I had a highway patrolman attend two of my personality type seminars. He raised his hand in the second seminar and told the group that he was a Promoter and after the first class he'd done a survey. He said he started noticing the personality types of people who ran out of gas. He stated the Promoters were big offenders because they didn't pay attention to details like where the gas gauge was pointing.

Some of the most interesting terms I've heard people use when referring to Promoters are: scatter-riffic, out-theres, chaos causers, clutter creators, space-cadets, larger than lifers, pieces of work, con-artists, and perpetual motion machines.

Key words that describe Promoters include:

Good News	Bad News
Articulate	Talkative
Charismatic	Superficial
Confident	Self-doubt
Encouraging	Fawning
Gregarious	Obnoxious
Persuasive	Overbearing
Playful	Childish
Optimistic	Unrealistic
Positive	Opinionated
Fun-Loving	Foolish
Brainstormer	Forgetful
Innovative	Disorganized
Flexible	Undisciplined
Inspiring	Poor Listener
Adaptable	Uncommitted
Spontaneous	Impulsive
Socially Skillful	Melodramatic
Friendly	Too Trusting
Cooperative	Inconsistent

The chart below is a summary of the major key characteristics of the Promoter personality.

PERSONALITY TYPE	PROMOTER
Roles:	Motivator
Motives:	Have fun, encourage people
Needs:	Attention Applause Recognition
Wants:	Relationships Freedom
Strengths:	Brainstorms Encourages Enthusiastic Charismatic Creative Articulate Optimistic
Limitations:	Disorganized Careless Impulsive Unrealistic Obnoxious
Focus on:	Possibilities and relationships
Adept at:	Understanding the aspirations of people
Abilities to:	Recruit and enlist
Communication: Tells = Direct Asks = Indirect	Direct Energetic Enthusiastic Tells stories Loud Interrupts

Likes environment to be :	Stimulating Fast-paced Congenial
Pluses about any job:	The Start The Challenge
Decisions are:	Spontaneous – from the Heart
Motto:	"Live, Laugh, Love" "Close Enough"
Fears:	Being bored Left out Unpopular
Stressors:	Rigid situations and people
When stressed:	Talks loud Obnoxious Impulsive Does shocking attention-getting things
Incompatible people:	Uptight, non-flexible, serious, boring, and narrow-minded
Compatible people:	Possibilities oriented, people oriented, having heart, enjoying life.
Good at:	Recruiting Enlisting Innovation Relationships Selling Encouraging others Inspiring others

CHAPTER 2

The Planners

Planner • Blue • Box

Personality Characteristics

Planners like orderly systems. They prefer all information in writing supported by charts and graphs. Planners like outlines. The following in outline form are the major characteristics of Planner personality types.

I. PERSONAL
II. WORK
III. SOCIAL

I. PERSONAL

    a. caring
    b. conforming
    c. conscientious
    d. conservative
    e. creative
    f. intimate
    g. honest
        1. high moral standards
        2. sincere
        3. has integrity
        4. guardian of truth

    h. loyal
    i. perfectionistic
    j. self-sacrificing
    k. sensible
    l. sensitive
    m. serious
    n. sincere
    o. thinker
    p. thoughtful
    q. traditional

II. WORK

a. accurate
b. analytical
c. careful
d. cautious
e. deliberate
f. dependable
g. detail-oriented
h. diligent
i. disciplined
j. dutiful
k. finisher
l. list-maker

m. hard-working
n. neat
o. no nonsense
p. organized
q. orderly
r. persistent
s. planner
t. problem-solver
u. punctual
v. quality oriented
w. scheduled
x. systematic

III. SOCIAL

a. compassionate
b. devoted
c. faithful
d. idealistic
e. realistic

f. respectful
g. self-sacrificing
h. sympathetic
i. unobtrusive

Needs

Affiliation

Planners are motivated by belonging and serving. They have a strong need for intimacy and affiliation with groups from the family unit to outside organizations. Planners are "joiners." Of special interest to them are service organizations, clubs that support charitable causes, as well as groups that uphold traditions and institutions. Scouting, veteran programs, politics, museums, libraries, church, and the family unit are listed among the Planner's favorites.

They need to be needed. They desire to serve and do their part. Planners are more comfortable as givers than receivers. They are selfless individuals. Find a service award program, and you'll find a Planner who founded it, a Planner who perpetuated it, and a Planner who won the award.

Honesty

Honesty is a hallmark of the Planner. These are usually the most moral, upright, honest, and sincere among us. They believe that everything should be done with integrity. This code of ethics guides most Planners in all of their decisions from business to social. Their word is their bond.

Quality

Quality in character, work, and leisure is important to Planners. The desire for perfection is strong in most of them. A favorite quote is, "A job worth doing is worth doing well." Traits like dependable, detail-oriented, serious, hard-working, deliberate, and thorough describe most Planners. They are known for the quality they bring to jobs, events, committees, teams, friendships, and families. Phrases like "Foundation of the Organization" and "Rock of Gibraltar" accurately describe these solid citizens.

Planners are deep people. Their strong desire to belong and serve, combined with their desire for perfection, makes them unique. At times they are not easily understood and can be perceived as critical and "nit pickers." As a rule, the other personality types do not have this perfectionist tendency.

Systems and Order

Planners like to play it safe. They want life to be predictable. That is why it is the Planners who write the rules, draw the maps, design the floor plans, and institute the procedure manuals. Planners must have a plan! "Make the plan and work the plan" is a slogan dear to the heart of a Planner. "A place for everything and everything in its place" is also sweet music to the ears of a Planner.

Planners place heavy emphasis on accuracy and objectivity. They make their decisions with their heads, trying to remain as unemotional as possible. They rely on data to solve problems. "The facts man, just the facts," is a favorite expression for Planners. They tend to be persistent in their analysis, maintaining a critical focus throughout the work or project. In a working environment they like order and clear guidelines. As workers they are independent, follow-through on tasks, and do well at technical jobs.

Planners like to take things one step at a time. These people move down the "yellow brick road" of life one brick at a time. They gather their information through their five senses. They know when they know something because they can see it, hear it, touch it, taste it, or smell it. This process of information gathering makes them very practical people. They are list makers who keep track of important dates like birthdays and anniversaries. Hallmark should get down on company knees and kiss the feet of these card-sending Planners.

Predictability

Change is not a favorite concept for Planners. Moves, job changes, and changing relationships can become near crisis situations. Status quo suits the ordered life of the Planner. They are not fond of impromptu and go with the flow situations. Flowing is just too spontaneous. Most Planners believe they can be spontaneous if given enough time.

Being given a surprise party for most Planners is a nightmare: no personal pre-planned agenda and no control because they did not personally organize it. "How much is this costing?" and "Where are the receipts?" are just a few of the questions darting in and out of their brains...not to mention some of the questionable guests. "Whose invitation list were they on, anyway?"

Under stress Planners tend to become quiet and continue to seek more information to increase confidence in their knowledge of the situation. This information seeking may hide their avoidance of an issue or their withdrawal from others. It may also delay decision-making. Some Planners can fall into the "analysis-paralysis" trap.

Because Planners are uncomfortable with emotions, they may try avoiding situations where they have to express emotions. They tend to put quality and accuracy ahead of feelings, even if it might hurt others. The Planner's strong desire for an orderly life causes family members, friends, and fellow workers to say: "Lighten up!" "Just go with the flow!" "Don't rain on my parade!" or "Please show some positive emotions."

One Planner told me the first time someone told him to "Lighten up and go smell the roses," he asked, "How many?"

Realism

Planners like things to be real. They paint their pictures with green grass and blue skies. Plants are meant to be real, and they have a difficult time with fake, make-shift, or substitutes. Planners stick with things the way they were meant to be. This group prefers not to wing it or make do. They want the right tool for the job.

This story entitled "Belts Are Suppose to Be Belts" makes the point.

I like to design clothes. Often I find myself mentally picturing an outfit in its completion. Early one evening last fall I saw in my head a dramatic black dress. Afraid I'd lose this mental picture, I raced around the house searching for things with which I could simulate the dress. I found an old faded black sheet and a Zorro cape in our costume box. Standing in front of the mirror with the black bed sheet pinned, taped, and hot glued around me I added the Zorro cape over one shoulder. Peering once more at the outfit in my mind, I noted the belt. It was about an inch wide, made of leather with a roll of silver nail head studs running down the middle. Upon closer scrutiny the belt looked much like a dog collar. Instantly, my mind flashed to the top shelf of my husband's office.

Although our beloved dog Madchen had been dead for twelve years, my Planner husband still had the collar. Racing down the hall with Zorro cape flapping, I retrieved the collar. Without breaking stride I tore through the kitchen. Grabbing the ice pick from a drawer, I whirled into the garage. I then laid the collar on the workbench, hammered the ice pick through the free end of the collar, and made a hole large enough to poke wire through. Threading the wire through the new hole, I dashed back upstairs to complete the design. Just as I was securing the wire to the buckle on the collar, my husband said, "Well, you are early for a change. Great, I need to make a stop before the dinner party."

In my designing frenzy I had used all the time I needed to dress for the evening creating my design. My decision about what to wear was made when I heard the garage door open and the car's motor start. I would have to hope no one noticed the glue. And I hoped that I remembered to navigate through the pins, that I kept the Zorro cape over the belt wiring mess in the back, and that I stayed in dimly lit corners. Throwing on a pair of wonderful earrings in an attempt to tie my creation together, I jumped in the car faded black bed sheet and all.

I have always operated under the assumption that it's my responsibility to fill all the drive time in the car with talk. After my husband briefed me on who's who of the other dinner guests, he went into his favorite car activity—silence. Reluctantly I participated in this activity for about three minutes. Then I was bored.

I decided it was my turn for my favorite activity, talking. I said, "Did you happen to notice my belt?"

Without removing his eyes from the road or his hands from the wheels, he said, "No." (Planners follow the rules—road signs, speed limits, seat belts buckled, hands on the wheel, and eyes on the road at all times.)

"Just take a quick glance over here because I want to tell you about it," I requested.

"Now, Vicki, you know I'm driving and can't take my eyes off the road," he stated.

"Walk on the wild side," I challenged.

He jerked his head my way in what I guess constituted a glance.

"Well, did you notice anything familiar?" I questioned.

"No, what is suppose to be familiar about your belt?" he asked suspiciously.

"I have on Madchen's old dog collar."

"Vicki, what if we are in an accident, and the paramedic notices you're wearing a dog collar for a belt?" he asked mortified.

"Fred, if we are in a terrible accident, the fact that I'm wearing a dog collar for a belt will be the least of my problems." Saying that, I laughed.

Some personality types can "wing it and make do," and others cannot. Planners like humans to wear belts and dogs to wear collars.

Tradition

Planners are very traditional. Holiday traditions are important. They don't want you changing the dressing and gravy recipe from the traditional recipe. Don't throw out all the old ornaments and get a new theme. And, please, put the tree in the same location where it has always been is the request of most planners.

They plan, ponder, and think about the things that become traditions. Traditions becomes rules. They like rules and conforming. This desire to do the right thing applies in the wardrobe area also. Of all the personality types, Planners are the ones who appreciate dress codes the most. Jobs that require wearing a uniform are agreeable for Planners. Their need for order gives then an understanding of concepts like standardization, compliance, and uniformity. Planners are generally no-nonsense, no-frills people. Uniforms are practical, hassle free, and economical, especially if the company provides them. All this adds up to a big plus for sensible Planners.

Creative in many areas, their desire to conform and be appropriate overrides any desire to use their creativity in the way they dress. Planners are concerned about the correct attire for each occasion. Being inappropriately dressed to a Planner would be rule-breaking and non-conforming, neither of which is acceptable. Most Planners are too conservative to add their own creative touch to an outfit. Often it is difficult for Planners to change the buttons or add a different belt. They stick to the way the manufacturer designed it. This is also the group that does not rip tags off of pillows and mattresses.

Conservative

Conservative by nature, Planners purchase in a low profile manner. Quality and price are important criteria for Planners. Most would rather have a few good things than a bunch of inexpensive choices. In clothes, they buy natural fabrics, straight-lined, traditionally styled garments that have been deemed always acceptable and appropriate. They generally like conservative colors, patterns, and styles. They select clothes that are basic, durable, and practical. Old standbys and tried and true garments appeal to this logical dresser. They enjoy sporty, preppie, and classic designs in their clothing. Twills, oxford cloth, tweeds, gabardines, and cottons are favorite fabrics for this group. Blazers with leather patches on the elbow, a button collar shirt, and a pleated skirt complete with loafers paints a classic traditional picture. No fads or gimmicks for this group.

Motives

Internal drivers for Planners are affiliation and belonging. They have a high need to belong, which includes emotional closeness or intimacy. This blue group seems to be a contradiction. They desire emotional closeness but also want everything to be right or as close to perfect as possible, and emotional closeness is often less than perfect. They move toward intimacy with high expectation. When their expectations are unmet, they retreat into isolation and lose what motivates them the most, intimacy and connecting.

Another strong motivator for this blue group is contributing to the organizations with which they are affiliated. Here comes another contradiction. Planners want to contribute, and they know the " best way" to do something. If they feel that others are doing it wrong, the blue group sometimes becomes intolerant and critical, thereby alienating people. Then contributing is a negative experience, and the sense of belonging is lost.

Planners seem to be able to keep track of friends better than any other personality type. They still communicate with grade school friends because they are organized and keep good address records. Planners seem to be the backbones of the class reunion committees. In this ability to keep track of relationships, we see the motive of belonging and connecting coming into play.

Good News – Bad News

First the good news. Planners really want to do things right. In business they discovered the "Best Practices" concepts. In life, if you want to know the most efficient way and often the cheapest way to do something, ask a Planner. Planners give a great deal of thought to the right way to do things. Then they can execute the plan, continually tweaking it for optimum effectiveness. Many in this blue group admit to being perfectionists. Doing it the right way is important to them.

Dependable, conscientious people are found in the blue group. These people are dutiful and diligent. Driven by their high need to serve, they are constantly worried that they didn't do their part. This group is the working backbone of most organizations. Others can and do count on Planners.

Planners like to problem-solve. It is a natural trait they possess. They are detail-oriented and thorough. Also, being very realistic, they tend to see the "down-side" or the "what can go wrong side." Planners are quality oriented problem solvers. But, how many problems can a person solve in one day?

The bad news is this group gets "used" by and to the advantage of others. Others know that Planners are afraid things will not get done or will fall through the cracks, so they count on these Planners and "dump" more responsibility on them. This group usually picks up the pieces and fixes the mess but not without resentment and grumbling. My Planner friend Carla says that if she could pick a new personality color, she would pick yellow. She's tired of being the dependable one while her Promoter husband has all the fun.

The blue group is the only group that wants things perfect. The yellow group says, "close enough—let's not make this boring." The red group says, "Do it my way, and get the job done now!" and the green group says, "Do it the easy way, but don't leave anyone out or hurt any one's feeling." So the blue group is in the perfectionist boat alone. And none of the other groups understand their compulsion to get it right.

Because the Planners are so realistic and think things all the way through, they tend to be perceived as "rainers on parades," or "carriers of doom and gloom." Often this group goes unappreciated. Then they become moody, depressed, withdrawn, and critical of others. Then everyone forgets all the great things the Planners accomplished.

Planners, here's something to ponder. As long as the rest of the personality types create "mess-ups," Planners will have problems to solve and will always feel needed and valued. So the question would be, is it good news or bad news that the other three personality types are not prone to perfectionism?

Key words that describe Planners include:

Good News	**Bad News**
Precise	Critical
Dependable	Obsessive
Steadfast	Stubborn
Systematic	Rigid
Cautious	Suspicious
Conscientious	Non-risking
Thorough	Excessive
Factual	Data bound
Creative	Moody
Methodical	Plodding
Dutiful	Guilt prone
Detailed	Nit-picky
Perfectionistic	Intense
Analytical	Analysis paralysis
Composed	Detached
Reserved	Unfriendly
Economical	Stingy
Realistic	Unimaginative

The chart below is a summary of the major key characteristics of the Planners personality.

PERSONALITY TYPE	PLANNER
Roles:	Problem-solver
Motives:	Belonging and contributing
Needs:	Appreciation Acceptance Order
Wants:	Accuracy Security
Strengths:	Integrity Organizer Sincere Reliable Practical Thoughtful Loyal
Limitations:	Self-righteous Perfectionistic Worries Moody Critical
Focus on:	Facts, tasks, and quality
Adept at:	Applying facts and experience
Abilities to:	Plan and problem solve
Communication: Tells = Direct Asks = Indirect	Indirect Detailed Factual Orderly messages Prefers written

Likes environment to be :	Organized Functional Practical
Pluses about the job:	The process Developing systems
Decisions are:	Calculated – Head
Mottoes:	"A place for everything and everything in its place." "Make a plan and work the plan." "Do it right the first time." "Those of you who think you know everything, really annoy those of us who do!"
Fears:	Making a mistake, compromising quality or standards, being mis-understood or dismissed emotionally
Stressors:	Change, chaos, sloppy work-manship, irresponsibility
When stressed:	Withdrawn, moody, cold, disengages. Goes back to facts and data for answers. Indecisive, develops "analysis paralysis." Holds onto old ways and things
Incompatible people:	Disorganized, insincere, inauthentic, and superficial
Compatible people:	Serious, dependable, intellectual, deep. Appreciative people

Good at:	Taking responsibility Getting things done Figuring things out Details Punctuality Quality performances Caring for the needy

CHAPTER 3

The Producers

Producer • Red • Check Mark

Producers are bold, results-oriented people. They take a direct approach to life. Producing results, achieving goals, and gaining power are strong motivators for Producers. They believe "time is money," and they like their information and communication to be bottom line and to the point. At no time do they like to have the point belabored. Producers like to "Get the show on the road." A general statement, followed by bullets, is their preferred written style.

Personality Characteristics

Producers are **Driven People.** Their drive to accomplish, combined with their desire to appear competent and knowledgeable in everything, is the force behind their behavior. Many Producers are:

- Optimistic and positive
- Resourceful and pragmatic
- Self-directed
- Self-motivated
- Disciplined about achieving goals

- Strong-willed
- Independent
- Self-sufficient
- Relentless pursuers of results
- Competitive
- Workaholics
- Performance addicts

Producers are **Task-Oriented.** The task, the job—the results, from a deadline being met to a building program being completed—these are the priorities of life for a Producer. However, they only produce results in the areas that interest them. They are take-charge people who are decisive and independent. Producers thrive on competition. They enjoy the challenge of a fight and enjoy the *win* even more. They are not afraid to take risks to get what they want.

They would rather make things happen than deal with people. Some Producers have a difficult time with personal relationships because they think of people as pawns to be used in order to complete the tasks. They possess strong leadership skills and have the ability to get people and projects moving forward to get things done. They usually wind up in leadership positions, regardless of the group or committee they are on. One of the reasons for this is because they are such excellent delegators. For the Producer, *doing* is more important than *being*.

Producers:

- Get things done
- Make things happen
- Like to get the show on the road
- Do things their way
- Get bored with anything that is not the big picture
- Need everyone to be competent and capable.

- Are not always in tune with people's feelings
- Manage projects better than personal relationships
- Like quick and practical solutions
- Set goals and believe benchmarks are key
- Are efficient and effective with time and materials
- Makes work paramount in life
- Are focused

Producers are **Leaders.** They manage things, projects, committees, teams, groups, and subordinates with efficiency, organization, and determination.

- Dynamic
- Self-confident
- Decisive
- Delegating
- Organizing
- Command Respect
- Possibility Oriented
- Strategic
- Visionaries

Producers are **usually correct** but are not always popular. They have intense personalities that evoke labels like:

- Shaker and Mover
- Crusader
- King of the Jungle
- Dynamo
- Dominating
- Aggressive
- Controlling
- Human Doing

Needs
Respect

Producers want and command respect. They drive themselves to "go the extra mile" in order to gain respect. They need to be seen as intelligent, knowledgeable, insightful, correct, competent, and skilled problem solvers. Their hot buttons are respect and admiration. Most Producers would choose to receive accolades for their accomplishments rather than for their acts of kindness.

One high paid executive told me he would rather have respect than be liked. I told him I thought both were possible if he decided that working on his people skills was a priority. The Producer is caught up in being perceived as confident, competent, and correct.

Competency in Everyone

Producers are sometimes guilty of the "Dumpster Syndrome." At any initial meeting of another person, Producers can make a snap decision about the person based on the following criteria:

- Is this person competent?
- Will this person be a good networking source?
- How can this person benefit my life?
- Can I learn anything from this person?
- Am I impressed with his or her credentials, demeanor, or appearance?

If the Producers count too many negatives with their personal rating system, then the "Dumpster Syndrome" goes into effect. Mentally, the Producers toss this type person out of their Rolodexes, out of their personal planners, out of their lives, and into a large mental dumpster because they have made the instantaneous decision that this one is not an asset to them. Motivated by the urge "to be done with that," Producers mentally trash people because clutter and excess are ineffective. Many Producers have found themselves digging frantically through their mental Dumpster to retrieve someone they were too quick too judge and found they later needed.

If the Producers' personal rating system seems somewhat harsh, remember that they require competency in themselves first, then in everyone else. Producers are their own strongest critics. They judge themselves based on their last accomplishment.

Leadership

Producers are born leaders who possess the characteristics and attributes needed to lead. They can rise to the occasion and handle the responsibilities that go with leading or being in charge. Their ability to make quick decisions, delegate, and problem solve are invaluable when solutions are needed in a hurry, which makes them good in emergency situations.

Being in charge often means calling the shots, and most Producers are comfortable calling the shots. This red group is, figuratively speaking, broad shouldered. You can find them out in front in most situations, carrying the major part of the responsibility load. They like responsibility and are good at handling challenging situations.

Being self-confident driven people, they want it done their way and preferably yesterday with speed and efficiency. And if you happen to be able to read a Producer's mind—that is good also.

Control

Producers read the parliamentary procedures books, study the rules for the game, learn foreign protocol, and know the pecking order at work. They are constantly networking and often take more than they give from their contacts. "Looking out for #1" is something they do well. Producers know "who's on first" and "what's going down." The reason why is not because they are consumed with a quest to gain knowledge for knowledge's sake. It is because the Producers believes knowledge is power.

If Producers know the rules to the game and their opponents don't, it gives them control. And they always want the power, control, or upper hand. Knowing more than anyone else gives them the leading edge. Producers like to be knowledgeable on everything—true walking encyclopedias. They believe "jack of all trades, master of some" is a good place to start. Then through specialized knowledge, along with understanding the dynamics of power and strategy, they continually rise to the top and master the rest.

Believing "knowledge is power," "a job well begun is half done," and "proper preparation prevents poor performance" serves them well. For Producers, life is a game, and they are playing to win!

When stressed Producers move from controlling to overbearing and dictatorial. Their need to accomplish causes them to push forward at all costs, giving little attention to details that may lead to mistakes. People and feelings may also be pushed aside. They become even more competitive, compulsive, and controlling when they don't think they are winning at the game of life.

Motives

Power and results motivate Producers. Webster's Dictionary defines power as the "possession of control, authority, or influence over others." In this definition is found the core of the Producer personality. These leaders, with their strong administrative skills, like power in their lives. They want authority positions, in jobs, projects, and activities/events whether large or small.

On one end of the spectrum are the Producers who use power and influence to accomplish wonderful achievements for many throughout the world. On the extreme other end of the spectrum are Producers who use power to dominate and control their world.

True to their name Producers, this group is about achieving results. Making it happen and getting it done motivate this group.

Good News – Bad News

Producers have great strengths and strong limitations or blind spots. The reason for such strong characteristics on both the good news side and bad news side is because our strengths taken too far become our weaknesses. For example most Producers have drive. But drive pushed to the extreme becomes obsession, compulsion, and performance addiction.

The good news is this red group is responsible for starting many great organizations, institutions, programs, projects, causes, and events. They see a need and do something about it. These "make it happen" specialists do just that! Producers are pragmatic. Whatever it takes to get the job done they will do.

The bad news is sometimes in their passion to achieve results and complete a project they forget certain details or how what is being accomplished is affecting people. Producers are big picture people who become extremely impatient when progress is deterred.

This group may have originated the saying, "Who do we have to kill to get the job done?"

A good news and bad news combination concerns being a super human doing verses being a great human being. Some Producers put so much emphasis on the doing side of life they forget to develop the character qualities. The Producers who say, "He who dies with the most toys wins," value achieving. You have to do well and make lots of money to buy the toys. Many Producers enjoyed varying degrees of financial success due to achieving in jobs and careers.

In the book, *We Are Driven,* by Dr. Robert Hemfelt, Dr. Frank Minirth, and Dr. Paul Mier is this description: "Humans *being* might jot down fifty chores on their things-to-do list, accomplish only four, and still feel satisfied with themselves. Humans *doing* can complete all fifty tasks and then spend the rest of the day wringing their hands wondering whether they performed well enough, or whether they were too easy on themselves and should have tackled sixty or sixty-five jobs instead of fifty."

The Golden Rule, "Do unto others as you would have others do unto you," involves character quality. You may or may not have achieved and accomplished results that buy material things, but you are a fabulous person. Some Producers enjoy good news across the board. They are fabulous human beings who are financially successful because the have been super human "doings." These people are what I call very "charactered" Producers. They have worked hard at developing their hearts.

Good News	Bad News
Posses strong task skills	May need to improve people skills
Decisive	Opinionated
Initiating	Controlling
Forceful	Abrasive
Driven	Impatient
Competitive	Arrogant
Goal oriented	Demanding
Authoritative	Dictatorial
Independent	Aloof
Pragmatic	Tactless
Productive	Hasty
Confident	Egotistic
Leadership ability	Bossy
Persuasive	Argumentative
Global	Selfish
Enterprising	Opportunistic
Focused	Self-absorbed

The chart below is a summary of the key characteristics of the Producers personality.

PERSONALITY TYPE	PRODUCER
Roles:	Leader
Motives:	Power and Results
Needs:	Approval Respect To be right
Wants:	Control Leadership
Strengths:	Decisive Doer Confident Competent Driven Vision Influential
Limitations:	Domineering Selfish Insensitive Manipulative Arrogant
Focus on:	Possibilities and Tasks
Adept at:	Developing concepts
Abilities to:	Accomplish and Achieve
Communication: Tells = Direct Asks = Indirect	Direct Authoritative Logical Bottom Line Unemotional

Likes environment to be :	Efficient Effective Productive
Pluses about the job:	Accomplishing the task Winning
Decisions are:	Decisive-Head
Motto:	"Time is Money" "I Want it Done Right the First Time"
Fears:	Loss of control Being seen as wrong or incompetent Loss of respect
Stressors:	Incompetent people Out of control situations Not producing enough
When stressed:	Verbal aggressive Domineering Manipulative Assertive Blunt Pushes harder for production
Incompatible people:	Lazy, Non-productive, Ineffective, Incompetents, Weak
Compatible people:	Other performers, Make it happen people, Self-assured, Competent
Good at:	Vision Strategies Making things happen Getting things done

CHAPTER 4

The Peacekeepers

Peacekeeper • Green • Oval

Personality Characteristics

Peacekeepers are considerate and value warm personal relationships. They have a strong sense of what people are feeling. They have a collaborative, cooperative style and enjoy being part of a team or family. Environments that place a high priority on teamwork suit them best. They are reliable and steady.

Peacekeepers don't want to control. However, they do not want to be controlled either. They enjoy life when everyone is "doing their own thing," especially them. They are independent, private, and reflective. Doing things in their own space and at their own pace suits them just fine. Although most of this group won't state this, many are thinking it, "Please get out of my space and out of my face!" They do not like demands placed on them. They are patient and tolerant with others and want the same in return. This green group originated the "everything in moderation" concept. They are middle of the road, moderate people who do not see the necessity of getting "all riled up." Life is meant to be lived at a slow pace. When pushed to produce or respond too rapidly this green group becomes overwhelmed and stubborn.

A strong belief in the value of each person plus the ability to admire and support the accomplishments of others make Peacekeepers desirable companions. The Peacekeepers' ability to support others often leads them to choose working in helping professions. They have good counseling skills. They are good listeners and clear thinkers but do not give advice unless they are asked.

Even though Peacekeepers lean toward independence, they make wonderful friends and can be valuable contributors to any organization. They are loyal, tactful, and thoughtful. Their easy-going nature makes them adaptable, agreeable people who are willing to please others. This quality makes it easy for them to get along with everyone. Diplomats of the finest order, when caught in the middle, they are able to remain neutral and open with both sides. Peacekeepers are skilled at negotiating and mediating because of their ability to understand and speak the language of all the personality types. Their balance and desire for right relationships lead them to their most important role of negotiator.

Peacekeepers promote harmony in any organization. They are motivated by peace and do not operate well in an atmosphere where animosity exists. This green group serves as anchors in the storms of life. They provide the calm in the troubled waters.

Needs

Acceptance

They accept others as they are and expect others to be accepting of them. Believing all people are created equal, they are known for their fair treatment of others. Kindness is key to them, both to be given and received. They focus on the good in people and situations. At times, their desire for unconditional acceptance makes it difficult for them to make decisions that may alienate one group or another. Their stand on acceptance makes them

"Rights' Crusaders." They march in parades promoting every-thing from children to animals' rights.

Respect

Peacekeepers cherish the right of the individual to be an indi-vidual, but they need others to affirm that they are worthy. Worthiness to Peacekeepers comes because they are human be-ings, and human beings should be respected. Respect for who they are, not what they do, is particularly important to this group. Respect for Peacekeepers is about feelings and human worth.

Peace

Wanting "peace at any price," they strive to avoid conflict and confrontation at all costs. Controversy is a Peacekeeper's nightmare. So to avoid it, they often keep their mouths shut, re-fraining from voicing objections or opinions. They are content when life is on an even keel and things are running smoothly. However, their desire for peace and harmony is so strong that they are sometimes willing to pay too high a price. They keep quiet or tell people what they want to hear in order to keep the peace. Passively putting up with unreasonable demands is some-thing they need to guard against. This conflict avoidance mode causes Peacekeepers to have their wants or needs go unmet. Of-ten these unmet needs and wants linger under the surface until they become resentments.

Those who do not understand the Peacekeepers may think they can continue to push these individuals. Their gentle demeanor may fool some, but eventually their stubborn will of iron sur-faces. This "get tough" behavior usually comes as a surprise to observers, but once their boundaries are infringed upon, they will usually let you know, in no uncertain terms, that a line has been crossed. Unfortunately, by this time it is probably too late for damage control.

Peacekeeper Tom was married to Helen the Blamer. For twenty-two years he stoically took the blame for everything from the weather to her health. One morning at 4:00 a.m. he went out to walk the dog. The dog returned. Tom never did. The attorneys handled the divorce, and Tom never spoke to Helen again.

Independence

Satisfied with solo activities such as reading, computer activities, playing a musical instrument, collecting, gardening, and working on hobbies or projects, Peacekeepers avoid "life in the fast lane." Content to stay quietly in the background, they don't need a lot of things or people in their lives. Most of the time, these private people keep their own thoughts and feelings to themselves. They are content to be alone much of the time in their personal pursuits. Simple pleasures and uncomplicated lives are more to their liking.

Balance

They are well-rounded individuals who are not prone to extremes, with an uncanny ability to balance work and play. Emotionally they stay pretty much on an even keel. They do not usually experience extreme highs and lows. This part of their make-up enables them to be cool under pressure. Calm, cool, and collected is an accurate way to describe these mellow people. In a working environment they want the work parceled out at a steady pace. Don't dump last minutes rushes and changes on this type if you can help it—piece out the work.

Motives

The driving force for Peacekeepers is peace, harmony, and balance in life situations and relationships. This group likes to be firmly grounded in life. They do not like life to be a juggling act or a hanging off the cliff experience.

My friend Richard, who owns a restaurant, recently shared with me that he had been offered an outstanding opportunity to increase his business and profits. He asked the investor, "Will this require me to stay in town the month of January instead of resting in Mexico as I do every January? The investor replied in the affirmative, and Richard said, "In that case, I don't want to increase my business or profit." Most peacekeepers are not driven and keeping balance in life, which supports peace, is their core motive.

Good News – Bad News

First the good news. Peacekeepers are universal friends. "What's not to like?" seems to be asked about the green group. Because of their caring hearts and gentle spirits, these people are usually easy to take and require low maintenance. They make their decisions through their hearts, considering the value of each individual. Harmony, balance, and peace are strong motivators in their decision-making process.

They have a high standard for themselves and others . Peacekeepers have high ideals about people and life situations. They are big fans of the human race and the endeavors of people.

This green group contains the eternal optimists when it comes to people. They try to see the hopes and dreams of others. They know how to hang in with people. These are the kindest human beings in the kingdom.

Because Peacekeepers like to avoid conflict they can learn to have amazing communication and conflict-resolution skills. It is usually after many negative experiences that these creative Peacekeepers decide "there must be a better way." Ironically, therefore, is it their distaste for conflict that pushes them to face conflicts head-on (before they become so large that this green group feels overwhelmed by them.)

Peacekeepers keep their heads when others about them are losing theirs. They can be calm in a crisis or in the general stress of day to day life. This status quo crowd likes to live life at a slow, steady pace. However, this group is plagued by what I call the "Whelms." If someone pushes the pace lever on their lives too high, they become overwhelmed. If you listen to the language of a Peacekeeper on the fast-paced track, you will hear lots of sighing and the word "overwhelmed" used frequently. This "peace at any price" group does not see an overloaded, fast- paced life as peaceful. They are patient, easy-going, non-confrontational people.

The bad news is because of their high standards, they are easily disillusioned and disappointed in people. The more stoic members of this green group keep their verbal "shoulds" and "oughts" to themselves. However, this silent disapproval can be poisonous.

Their kindness is often mistaken for weakness. They can be over-trusting and gullible. This can be a reason why some Peacekeepers become the victims of scams and cons.

They sometimes hang in when the hopes are gone and the dreams cannot come true. This group takes a long time to give up on others. There is always the hope for them that tomorrow it will be different. Sometimes it is, sometimes it isn't. Some Greens tend to stay in unhealthy relationships too long. Their ability to tolerate others, coupled with their tendency to avoid conflict, sometimes prevents this green group from receiving what they need in a relationship. They are willing to give and give without receiving for a long time. BUT—remember this, when these Peacekeepers are pushed to their limit, they are capable of walking away from a relationship and not looking back. They are often unwilling to seek counseling or consider reconciliation at this point.

Because Peacekeepers don't want to confront they can be passive resistive and passive aggressive.

My walking friend, Lynn, is a gentle Peacekeeper, and she is married to a controlling man I call Robert the Red. Last Christmas, Robert the Red gave Lynn a beeper for which only he had the number. The day after Christmas as we were walking along the oceanfront her beeper went off. Panicked, we raced to the pay phones near the pier. Neither of us had any money, but I had my phone credit card number memorized. She used that number to respond to the emergency. The emergency was: "Where was the morning newspaper?"

The second emergency dealt with a misplaced shirt, the third involved the location of his car keys, and the fourth was a demand that she shorten her walk and come home. As we continued toward our planned destination the beeper went off for the fifth time. Lynn reached down and removed it from her waistband and, without missing a beat, dropped it into the first trash receptacle we passed.

I said, "Lynn, Robert the Red will kill you!"

She said, "No, he won't. He'll buy me another beeper. That one I'll leave out so Mutt, his beloved dog, can chew it up. The third one I'll let our granddaughter Katie drop in the toilet. By the time he gets me the fourth one, I'll have its demise figured out, too."

I asked, "I guess confronting is out of the question?"

She laughed and said, "Vicki, you of all people should know I'm going to take the line of least resistance. I would rather solve this situation by being passive than active. And believe me, he will wear down sooner than I do. I will win this battle in my own quiet way."

She never had to figure that one out because after the third beeper, the beepers stopped coming.

Key words that describe Peacekeepers include:

Good News	Bad News
Balanced	Overwhelmed
Accommodating	Lenient
Tolerant	Indulgent
Patient	Push-over
Kind	Sentimental
Good Listener	Co-dependent
Easy-going	Complacent
Calm	Unenthusiastic
Sympathetic	Timid
Moderate	Unmotivated
Diplomatic	Indecisive
Steady	Hesitant
Accommodating	Passive Resistive
Independent	Uninvolved
Responsive	Over-committed
Inoffensive	Weak
Practical	Avoids
Laid back	Lazy

The chart below is a summary of the major key characteristics of the Peacekeeper Personality.

PERSONALITY TYPE	PEACEKEEPER
Roles:	Diplomat
Motives:	Peace and Balance
Needs:	Acceptance Respect Independence
Wants:	Stability Contentment
Strengths:	Clarity Listens Diplomatic Kind Patient Moderate Adaptable Peaceful Tolerant Balanced
Limitations:	Indecisive Unmotivated Overly sensitive Stubborn Unproductive Overwhelmed Submissive Uninvolved
Focus on:	Facts and Relationships
Adept at:	Meeting daily concerns of people
Abilities to:	Collaborate and Mediate
Communication: Tells = Direct Asks = Indirect	Indirect Empathetic With clarity Calm and Collected Hesitant to speak up

Likes environment to be :	Friendly Casual Open door policy
Pluses about the job:	The Involvement Relationships
Decisions are:	Consultative-Heart
Motto:	"Peace at any price" "Don't make waves"
Fears:	Major life change, Major personal problems, Overwhelming life circumstances being handled alone
Stressors:	Fast pace, Disharmony Conflict, Instability
When stressed:	Avoids-Isolates "Veges-out," Denies, is Lazy, Becomes a couch potato Distractions from the problem— TV, books, sleep Manual activities—woodwork, knitting, crafts
Incompatible people:	Controlling, Pushy, Loud, Domineering, Demanding
Compatible people:	Collaborative and supportive Helpmates for decisions Respect them for who they are, not what they do
Good at:	Keeping the peace Showing compassion Staying calm Listening Finding balance Friendships

Two Personalities in One

A commonly asked question I receive as I travel around conducting seminars is: Can you be two personality types? I answer, "I believe God created us with one core personality. He made each of us our own unique shade of whatever color our core type may be. But I also know from myself and from talking with thousands of people in my seminars, many of us have a second personality type that comes right along side of our core type. My core is Promoter, but I wear my red Producer shirt much of the time."

One day I started out wearing my Promoter shirt. I was rushing to get to a fund raising luncheon where I was the guest speaker. I jumped into my car, started the engine, and the gas level warning light blinked. So I grabbed my son's car keys. My son drove a beat-up old van with the spare tire hanging off the back.

After the luncheon I was driving down the street, and the light changed to yellow. I knew that gunning the van was not an option, so I stopped abruptly. In the next second a large Mack truck lightly tapped the rear of the van. I was not hurt, but two things happened on impact. First, the spare tire fell off the van and went rolling across two lanes of traffic, over the center divider, and flopped over dead in the fast lane of the oncoming traffic. Second, the heel of my very high-heeled shoe broke off. As I got out of the van to look at the damage, I was walking with a very pronounced limp.

The driver, who seemed the size of a giant, stormed out of his truck shouting, "Listen lady, that was clearly your fault. I hope when my company calls you that you will have the decency to tell them it was your fault."

This is when I threw on my red Producer shirt! I responded with, "Thank you for asking. You'll be glad to know I'm not hurt." Before he could speak, I spun around and started limping across traffic toward my tire.

In the center divider, he caught up and grabbed me by the arm and said, "Hey lady, I don't think you know what you're doing. You'll never get that tire out of there alone." Then he looked down at my hands and stated, "Besides you'll break one of them there pretty finger nails."

Because he was huge, I decided not to correct his grammar. I stood up tall and said, "I am in complete control of this situation. I most certainly do not need your help." With that he laughed, strolled back, and leaned on his truck to watch.

The truth was I did need help. It was a very windy day, and I had on a full skirt, which was blowing all over the place. I did not realize how heavy a dead tire can be. While watching traffic and trying to hold down my dress, I struggled with the tire. By shear determination I finally got it standing up. As I rolled and limped toward my van, the huge man glared at me.

As I neared my van the next challenge hit me. How would I get this heavy tire into the van? As I rolled in front of him he sneered, "Good luck." By now I was angry and fearful of losing control. But the sneering comment shot up my adrenaline response. I yanked open the sliding door, rolled the tire up my leg, used my leg like a forklift, and shoved the tire in the van. I slammed the door shut, stormed back, and took down the "How am I driving?" number off the back of his truck. Finally sitting behind the wheel of my van I let out a big sigh. I had a ruined dress, four bleeding fingernails, and a broken shoe. But I had taken control and gotten the job done, wearing my red Producers tee shirt with determination and perseverance.

SECTION TWO

The KIDS

The KIDS

Have you ever thought:

- This child is not at all like me.
- Where did this kid come from?
- How can kids raised in the same family be so different?
- I'm not like that at all.
- I'd never do it that way.
- I don't understand this child!

This section will respond to these thoughts and questions. Since there is no one exactly like you, no one of the exact hue as you, why is it so difficult to accept that none of the children in your life are just like you? It is not our similarities that cause most of the frustration when working with children; it is the differences. Learning about the personalities of the children in your life and knowing your core personality helps you to understand and improve the quality of those relationships.

As I speak to audiences of parents and teachers, they find it easy to identify the Promoter and Producer children. The Planners and the Peacekeepers often take a bit more analyzing. The child you are trying to understand may wear not one but two tee shirts rather consistently. This a factor is to be considered.

If you have very young children, you may not be able to identify their personality types just yet. However, many of my friends are grandmothers, and most of them know their grandchildren's personality types around the first year. Gramma Standley said, "Our newest grandbaby is definitely a Producer. He gives us a look that says, 'Enjoy being in charge while you can, soon I'm taking over.'"

Another grandmother Nana Nelson reported, "Joshua is for sure a Planner, his Tonka™ trucks are always lined in a perfectly straight line across the room, and he does not like them to get out of order. I have ten grandchildren, and this one at three is the most orderly and serious of them all."

My friend, Sharon, described her week of babysitting for her three grandchildren like this. "Well, Alex was her usual in-charge Producer self. I'm sure that girl is going to be President some day. T.J. entertained me all week with his wild stories and sparkling Promoter personality. I know baby Cameron is a Peacekeeper. I've never seen a more docile contented baby in my life."

A letter came from a seminar participant, Planner Kimberly, a fourth-grade teacher. It read as follows:

> After your seminar I took the picture of the four personality type tee shirts to school. I taped it to my desk. Some of my students I immediately identified and wrote their names by the appropriate shirt. Over the weekend I studied your handouts and was able to identify almost all of my class. I wrote their names by the shirt they wore the most. There were still four children about whom I was confused. In the week that followed your seminar I paid special attention to my unidentified four. Two I finally figured out were Planners, but since both of them had rather disorganized desks much of the time, they stumped me for a while. When I questioned Carrie about the messy desk I knew she was a Planner. She said, "I want a clean

desk. I want it perfect. I hate things messy. I have a big desk at home, and I keep it just right. But this one is too small, and there are too many books and things to fit right so I just gave up."

My last two unidentified students were born drug babies and come from horrendous backgrounds. Each has severe emotional problems. I remember you said that children like this were often difficult, if not impossible, to identify. These two need all the love and understanding they can get. I'll keep working on it.

Thank you on behalf of the children. Your seminar really helped me to do a better job with each individual personality in my class. I know this is a Planner thing, but I've even listed what I think are shades of their group colors.

As you read this section with specific children in mind, remember to rule out personalities that don't fit the child. As you continue and finish this book keep a list of certain personality characteristics that fit the child you are trying to identify. At the end, most of you will know the personality type or the tee shirt the child you are thinking about wears most of the time.

HUG ME, I need affection!

CHAPTER 5

Perky Promoters

Perky Promoter • Yellow • Spring

My friend Linda, a pediatric hospital nurse, said she can usually spot this personality group even in the newborn section. She claimed there is a perky attitude and energy for the joy of life in these newborns. Laughingly she said, "It's like they are looking at me and saying, 'Hey, this life stuff is great! Aren't you glad I'm here?'" Perky Promoters like life and themselves unless someone convinces them of the contrary.

Linda summed up Perky Promoter children well. They have a zest for life that spills energy and joy to those around them. They have a beckoning call to join them. Life is for living—let the fun begin.

My girlfriend, Diane, described her eighteen-month old Promoter Grandson this way. When Collin's Mom is away and she calls to talk to him, because he has no verbal language to communicate with her, upon hearing her voice, he puts the phone down and wiggles his whole body with joy.

My friend, Phil, describes his yellow son Cole who is six in this way. "Cole brings joy to the end of my workday. He stands in the driveway, and the minute he sees my car, he does the dance of football players in the end zone and yells, 'Daddy's home, yeah!'

Cole has a gusto about him that says: Life is to be lived to the fullest. Let's not miss anything."

The Perky Promoters are busy, animated, fast-paced children. Their activities are often random and scattered. These children are easily distracted because life is so wondrous, and they do not want to miss a thing. For this yellow group life is to be experienced in an all-out, go for the gusto blitz. They want to take everyone they encounter along for the ride. These are free spirited children. They have huge imaginations and the courage to risk and go for it. This group isn't always sure where they are going, but they are going. They represent the saying, "I don't know where I'm going but I'm making great time!"

These are highly verbal children. They like words and are usually very articulate even as small children. Their gifts of having big hearts and loving people help them express their emotions and feelings. And these children have strong emotions and feel deeply! They have a sixth sense about people around them. These children express what they are feeling and what others might be feeling. Promoters are often very candid and tell it like it is. They don't always act on what they feel, but they will express it. Often these children are better talkers than doers.

An idea a minutes pops into the heads of these children. They are great at brainstorming and thinking up wild and crazy schemes. Some are better at implementing than others. Starting is fun. They can rise to the challenge and thrill. They start something, figure out: "Hey I can do this," and stop. They stop because now "they've been there and done that." They have met the challenge, and that's enough for them. Ideas are their specialty, starts are next, and finishes are last for most of this group. Mastery is unimportant. Often completion seems boring and repetitious, and these children do not do anything boring if they can help it.

Following through can be difficult for these children. Several factors come into play here:

- High energy
- Not liking routine or repetition
- Having too many ideas to focus on one
- So busy experiencing and promoting life, they can't stay in one place too long
- They bore easily and can be impulsive
- Running the race of life is a sprint not a marathon for Perky Promoters.

In one of my seminars recently, a mother rushed up afterwards and said, "Last week I had my child tested to see if she had Attention Deficit Disorder or was Hyper-Active. The test said she was neither. I still wondered what was wrong with her. She is so active, unfocused, and all over the place. Now I know there is absolutely nothing wrong with her. She is a very bright yellow Promoter."

Adults Need to Understand This About Perky Promoters:

We Like Life to be Fun.

For Emotional Growth We Need Lots of A's:
- Attention – Watch me, listen to me.
- Approval – Did I do "good"? I need to know.
- Affection – I'm a kid who operates with my heart. Hug me, Love me.
- Audience – Please watch me play out my life.
- Applause – I'm a performer. I need to see and hear your approval.
- Acceptance – Don't leave me out! I must be included.
- Affirmations – Keep telling me how wonderful I am. I live for praise.

Our Specialties:
- Having a good time
- Helping others to have a good time

- Encouraging others to reach full potential
- Talking to anyone about anything
- Bubbling personality
- Entertaining people
- Funny
- Fun friend
- Giving compelling reason to get what we want
- Considering others' feelings

What Makes Us Sad:
- Being left out
- Thinking no one likes us
- People who say mean things about us
- Mean people
- Being yelled at for not having our "act together"
- Losing things, and we do it a lot!

Fears:
- Not being popular
- Strict rules
- Being bored
- No freedom
- No fun
- No friends
- Mean people

What Is Fun for Us:
- Doing things with friends
- Talking to friends at school or on the phone
- Just being with our friends
- Vacation with our family and other families with kids
- Special trips with friends
- Birthday parties, especially our own
- Getting to do special things like performing in plays and shows
- Being on teams that go for pizza after the game

Help Us with:
- Organizing time and materials
- Being too optimistic
- Being too gullible
- Being too accepting
- Emotionally flying all over the place
- Telling the truth
- Planning ahead

Attention Grown-ups: This Is Important Stuff!

Needs

Attention

These children need more attention than most parents realize. They never can hear enough words of encouragement or praise. This group is like puppies jumping around your ankles waiting for you to pat them on the head and say "atta" girl or "atta" boy, just because they exist. Promoters need lots of pats on the head for encouragement and hugs to keep them going. Affirmations that say they are good and that you love them, not for what they do but because they exist, are music to their ears.

Because this group is not as task-oriented as they are relationship-oriented, as parents you may have to focus your praise on their character qualities versus their performances and results. Mention their character qualities such as friendliness, generosity, including others, humor, optimism, and how much fun you have with them. Please don't hold back your words of affirmation until your child performs a home task or a school task well. This child thrives on praise. Verbal affirmations are vital to meeting the attention needs for this child.

All children say, "Watch me, Mommy, Watch me, Daddy." But this group needs an audience as they unfold their life drama. Most of these children like spotlight time where they can be the center of attention. Many of these children have a great sense of humor. Some are comedians. Parents describe these kids as "hams," "cut-ups," thespians, or clowns. You can often find the class clown among this group. They entertain everyone and definitely get an A in social life.

As an elementary school teacher I found the yellow group generally liked "Show and Tell." They always had something to say. I call this story "A Star Is Born."

Charlynn was a charming, bright yellow Promoter. She was in my Kindergarten class. At six years of age, life was a play, and she held the starring role. For Charlynn the "Show and Tell" time was her forum. I knew I could always count on Charlynn to have something to say. She was naturally articulate, and at a tender age, knew how to hold the attention of an audience. Promoters are naturally good storytellers. Charlynn had a very big imagination. She made her family and her dog Muffin larger than life. To hear Charlynn share her glamorous family life, you would think it was a movie script. When in fact, it was just a normal average family with a below average dog. She used her charming wit to transform the ordinary into the extraordinary.

One of my challenges as her teacher was to help her separate fact from fiction. Promoting children can inflate and exaggerate stories to make them more exciting and make themselves look more important than they are. Image is important to some Promoter children. Sometimes they will even resort to lying to make things bigger and more important than they are. This personality group has a strong awareness of social standing and status.

Usually Promoters are easy to spot. They are not only highly verbal and vocal, they are also visual. They will be seen animatedly moving with sweeping gestures and often wearing the latest style with flash and pizzazz. This group has flair and panache. Most are not shy about standing out in a crowd. Often that is precisely their motive. They like to be in style. Cutting-edge fashions and brand-name clothing are important to most of these children and teenagers.

Popularity

Yellow group children are people magnets. They have a "come one, come all" attitude and "more is always merrier." They are Pied Pipers because the music of their lives is lively, upbeat, and invites others to join in the merriment. Engaging and entertaining, they are great at influencing others to join in their work or play. Think about Tom Sawyer and Huck Finn. Who watched and munched on an apple while his friend took over the painting?

Our friends, Planner Don and Peacekeeper Ann laughingly describe being the parents of a Promoter. "From a very early age Josh had a lot happening. Because of him our house was a hive of activity. The phone rang more for him than for anyone else. Most of the knocking at the door was for Josh. He always had twice as many friends around as our other kids." Josh was a busy boy with an active social life to maintain.

Our son Tyler is also a perky Promoter. As a young child people called him "Tyler the Smiler." Plus he is a charmer. He had developed social skills very young and was always at ease with adult as well as peers. He charmed his way into everyone's heart. There was always an upbeat energy when Tyler was around.

When Tyler was in elementary school I used to wait until he got home to run the boring errands. When he was with me it turned boring into to a fun adventure. He pointed out things I had never seen before. He helped me laugh at myself on those "whatever can go wrong will go wrong" days. It seemed I was always the one who got the shopping cart with the loud crazy wheel or the leaky carton of milk. If anyone was going to drop a carton of eggs on brand new shoes, it was me.

We were so much alike it was a great time for me to show him the good news and the bad news about being who we were. However, as he got older, one-on-one time with Tyler was rare. His friends were always around or calling. As a teenager it seemed to our family that his friends were his life.

Relationships, especially with peers, are often more important than anything else to these children. Friendships and popularity are high on the list for Promoters. School for this group is first about interacting with their friends often with the academics coming in second.

Parents of Perky Promoters state that perky isn't 100 percent. These upbeat children can roller coaster from on top of the world to the bottom in record time. Often the trigger point is criticism, exclusion, or a perceived slight by a friend. Fortunately, like the roller coaster, their downs might be deep but usually not long.

Carrie is a darling, yellow teenager. She has so many boyfriends, I can't keep up. I asked her mother if Carrie is always the heart breaker. Her mom said it's about 50/50. The cycle is one minute this is "Mr. Right," and the next minute her heart is broken, followed by dramatic tears and, of course, a new boyfriend. Life is again a joyous happening. Her dad says her theme song is, "If You Can't Be with the One You Love, Then Love the One You're With."

Flexiblity

A spring is flexible, and Promoter children and teenagers want flexibility in their lives. From meals to rules to school, this group wants versatility. This group likes to reinvent the wheel. They often do something a different way each time. Tight boundaries and rigid rules are very difficult for this group to follow.

The teen years can be difficult for parents and these children. After all, this yellow group believes rules are made to be broken. Because life is meant to be fun and peer relationships are at the top of their priority list, then it follows that schoolwork and chores at home barely make the list—and certainly not as priorities. Some of these children are just plain wild. They are going to experience life and all it brings. Hedonistic, narcissistic, and out of control behavior can happen to some of these kids. The family takes the brunt of their ugly behavior while they use their charm on everyone else.

Once the difficult years are over, these Promoters will again bring their joy and energy back to the family. Relationships are paramount to Promoters. They need family and friends.

Good News	Bad News
Charming	They can be phony and cunning
Entertaining Storytellers	Beware of minnows that suddenly grow into whales as the story progresses
Flexible	Too loose to contain–mercurial
Positive and Optimistic	Unrealistic dreamer
Friendly	Self-serving, using popularity to get what they want
Enthusiastic Volunteer	Uncommitted, unreliable–drops the ball
Creative Ideas	No focus or follow through
Delightful	More fluff than substance
Fun-loving	Shallow and foolish
Spontaneous	Impulsive and forgetful
Unique	Nonconforming
Excellent Communication Skills	Non-stop talking

Teenage Promoters

<u>Good News</u>	<u>Bad News</u>
Fun	Friends are more important than family
Cheerleader of Life	Wild Child
Joyful	Rebellious toward rules and boundries
Energetic	Total Flake
Charming	If it feels good do it
Encourager	Rebellious in appearance
Magnetism	Vain
Hangout House	Enlist the whole family in their life
Social Whirl	Grabbing all the attention and hogging the spotlight
Fast-paced	Exhausting for others to be around

Have I got a story to tell you!

You don't understand how bad I feel when I don't get it right.

PLANNER

CHAPTER 6

Precise Planners

Precise Planner • Blue • Box

As a teacher most Planner children were a blessing to have in my classroom. These are dependable, dutiful, responsible children. Even the ones who struggled academically were good kids, diligently taking it one step at a time, trying to get it right.

On the whole this blue group were not discipline problems. Rebellion in school would go against their conforming, rule-following nature. Are Planners perfect angels all the time in school? No, but the format of school is usually a comfort zone for these children and an arena that meets many of their needs, so they fit.

They like the routine of the daily schedule. Things are put in writing, and they know what's expected of them. These children like a life that is systemic and orderly, and school is generally one of those places. The consistency of the school day appeals to these boundary-desiring children.

Planners don't like to be late. Tardiness for this group represents breaking rules, irresponsibility, and disorganization. All traits that go against the grain of these "by the book" children.

Planner children as a group manage time and materials very well. The neatest desk awards usually goes to students in this group. They don't like clutter, chaos, or things out of place. This group coined the phrase "a place for everything and everything in its place." And most of them stick to it. At the end of the year these students still had all twenty-four crayons in the twenty-four pack, and few were broken. Whereas the Promoters were down to several broken stubs of the less desirable colors.

Precise Planners can take their strong desire to get it right to the next level—perfectionism. Being analytical and detailed-oriented these kids know what "right" should look like. The logical voice in their heads says, "Getting life right all the time is not possible." But many in this group still have to give it their best shot.

There are seemingly opposing goals in both the adult and child version of the Planner. On one side there is a strong desire for perfection, but on the other their logic-based minds say, "It can't happen." Perfection and pessimism seem to surround Planners. Frustration, discouragement, and negativity are common feelings for these children. They want to get it perfect, but history, their own data, and logic say it won't happen. So enters "gloom and doom time." Tapes in their heads that say, "I'll never get it right. I'm a huge failure." These are the "black clouds overhead" times that Planners experience.

Tears of frustration poured over six- years-old Randy's chubby cheeks. He had spent the whole morning learning to tie his shoes. He had finally mastered the bow but the laces wouldn't stay tied. Standing in the kitchen with not one but two untied shoes, he declared that, " life was just not fair," and stormed into his bedroom.

I asked his mother how she was going to handle it, and she said, "I'm not. He'll stay in his room having a pity party and then he will finish that and start trying again to tie the perfect bow. This child is tightly and intensely made. His day is a roller coaster of emotions. He is caught between his perfectionism and his pessimism. He sets his standards so high that when he fails it's the end of the world. Poor Randy, I hope he finds middle ground soon."

Tightly and intensely made is a good description for many in this group. From the homework papers that aren't neat enough, to projects that don't turn out perfectly, these children set high standards for themselves. They put pressure on themselves and become upset and discouraged when things don't turn out the way they had planned.

Planners work and play intensely. Toys or activities with many parts and details appeal to Planners. They have the ability to focus and really stick with a project, becoming absorbed and oblivious of the world around them. Liking the process and enjoying developing systems, they like playing with toys with lots of pieces—Legos™, puzzles, tinker toy, and erector sets. Girls like the whole kitchen, complete with every dish, appliance, and pan. Barbie's accessories are usually more enjoyable for this blue group than Barbie.

Adults Need to Understand This about Precise Planners:

We Like a Life Where Things Are Right, with as Few Mistakes and Goofs as Possible.

For Emotional Growth We Need:
- Appreciation for the way we think it through and try to get it right
- Appreciation for quality work
- Appreciation for being responsible
- To belong
- Acceptance in groups
- Stability
- Security
- A game plan

Our Specialties Are:
- Organizations
- Solving problems with practical solutions
- High standards and ideals
- Thoughtfulness

- Dependability
- Honesty
- Following rules
- Independent thinking

What Makes Us Sad or Mad:
- Craziness in life
- When people don't do it right, like cheating and sloppiness
- When no one seems to care about correcting things
- Flakes, goof-offs, and lazy people
- Disorganization

Fears:
- Making mistakes
- Not being understood
- Not being accepted
- Having to do something poorly or only half-way
- Having other people play with or touch our things and mess them up

What Is Enjoyable for Us:
- Vacations with our families
- Friends doing something together
- Going to clubs and groups where it's organized and with opportunities for projects and earning awards
- Working on a project in a place where we have space
- Sometimes school
- Some sports teams but not with a lot of kids that just want to mess around

Help Us with:
- Overcoming negativity
- Finding the positive things is life
- Flexibility
- Seeing what is right about a situation versus what's wrong
- Increasing our tolerance of others
- Being less rigid

Attention Grown-ups: This Is Important Stuff!

Needs

Order, Planning and Routine

My friend Anne is a single mom. She and her son (twelve) and daughter (ten) are all Precise Planners. Visiting their home anytime, day or night, is amazing. The house looks magazine perfect, and no matter what activity they are engaged in there is no mess. At Halloween they carve pumpkins and make candy apples without seeds and sticky on the floor. They dye Easter eggs without colored stains anywhere, and even Christmas morning the living room doesn't look like a hurricane ripped through.

Anne says her hardest job as a parent to these Planner kids is not to make them do things right, but to encourage them to lighten up and let their standards have some flexibility. She states, "My children put way more pressure on themselves to get it right than I ever would put on them. I'm an up-tight Planner, too, but I've had to loosen-up because my two kids are both such perfectionists. Someone around here has to lighten up and go with the flow."

Going with the flow is often hard for Planners because flowing is just too spontaneous and risky. Most Planners don't like change and aren't too excited about a lot of risky situations. "Make a plan, and work the plan," fits most blue group lifestyles. Planners claim they can be spontaneous if you give them enough time!

Being Part of the System

Planners need for order comes into play in their need to be part of systems. Organizations that have structure, rules, charts or guidelines that tell them exactly what to do and how to do it appeal to this group. Blue group children actually like directions on a box, and they read them. In an attempt to get it right this groups believes that directions might help. A systematic organization like Scouting or Camp Fire Girls attracts Planners.

Belonging to an organization, a family, a school, a church or synagogue, and a community meets the needs for affiliation in these children. They like being members of things. Planner children are the backbones of organizations. They are the ones who attend regularly and do the work it takes to move to the next level. They are often the group leader's dream participants. They follow the rules, do their part, and then some. Planners are servants at heart—hard workers who would not dream of letting others carry their share of the load. You can count on planners to do their part and do it well.

The three boys I know who have attained the honor of Eagle Scout are all blues. The last two bar mitzvahs and one bas mitzvah I know about were all from the blue group. These accomplishments take determination, dependability, and stick-to-itiveness, and this group has it. They thrive on being part of an organized system.

To be Appreciated

Remember you are dealing with perfectionists, precise Planners. They don't like to generalize about or round off anything. Affirm them, praise them, and let them know how much you appreciate them in an exact and precise manner. Planners love things in writing. When putting it in writing, be specific. Give details, focus on quality, and describe the when, where, why, and how of exactly what you appreciate about your Planner child.

This group likes the past. History is very important to them, and so is personal history. Create it for them with keepsakes, photo albums, cards, and notes that will become part of their history.

My sister is a Planner. As children we shared a room. She saved stuff—the napkin from her first Brownie Tea, report cards, and awards. Every note, Valentine, and corsage she ever received was neatly and carefully filed, pasted, or pressed into the living memories of her life. Her side of the room reflected who she was. Bookcases, window ledges, and her bedside table created her history and portrayed a deep, caring, and organized young woman.

My side was a chaotic disaster. Being a fast moving Promoter, I winged it as I went along. What I didn't lose, I destroyed or tossed. I had no time or organizational skills to mess with stuff. My saving methods consisted of shoving it under my bed.

Your Planner child is deep. They are trying to get life "right." Let them know that you know this about them, and you love and appreciate who they are.

Good News	Bad News
Dependable and thorough	Can be slow
Can read a manual and figure out how to fix things	Have to assemble the perfect equipment to do the job first–this can take days!
Sets Goals	Makes too many and sets too high of standards
Punctual	Gets stressed when others are late
Deliberate	Not spontaneous
Dutiful	Sensitive if not appreciated
Sincere	Too sensitive–hurt by insincerity
Problem solvers	Indecisive–analysis paralysis
Practical	Doesn't like a lot of new ideas
Deep	Moody
Makes few mistakes	Critical of others' mistakes
Realistic	Pessimistic
Perfectionist	Perfectionist

Teenage Planners

Good News	Bad News
Organized	Inflexible
Trustworthy	Secretive
Serious student	Puts way to much pressure on self— "all work, no play"
Determined	Disappointed in their own performance
Steady	Self-critical
Observer	Withdrawn
Thoughtful	Hurt by insincere people
Sensible	Nerds
Responsible	Old fashioned
Quality person	Goodie-Goodie
Traditional	Hangs on to clothes even when they are old and worn

You can count on me. I'll do it!

I like proving I can do something you said I couldn't make happen!

CHAPTER 7

Powerful Producers
Powerful Producer • Red • Check Mark

It might have been the pain or maybe the drugs when our Powerful Producer son Matt was born, but this is what seemed to happen. His birth had been painful. Maybe it was because he was born in a three-piece suit carrying a briefcase. He seemed to immediately take charge of the delivery room, demanding to see the credentials of all the medical staff. Somewhat satisfied with their abilities to get the results he wanted, he turned to us, the parents. Looking at us with skeptical eyes that said, "Huh! I knew it. I got born to a couple of incompetents. But no problem, I'm in control here, I can shape them up in no time." He's been trying for twenty-seven years.

Raising Powerful Producers is the best of times and the worst of times. The Bible says, "Unto whom much is given much is required." These children have incredibly strong strengths and equally strong blind spots. Generally, this red group puts pressure on themselves first and then everyone else. They are driven, and they are taking themselves and everyone in their lives along for the ride. The ride isn't usually a joyride. No aimless running around the countryside for this group. Producers try not to aimlessly go anywhere, and they rarely spin their wheels. They set goals and go for the win. These children are like racecars, driving in the fast lanes of the freeways of life and pressing for the finish line.

Producers are purposeful children. Accomplishments, achievements, and results are important to them. They are also very competitive. In early elementary school, recess games, spelling bees, and test grades give them a chance to compete and win. Later it is sporting teams, debate team, or the grade chase that challenges them to compete with winning in mind. Producer Vince Lombardi summed it up for this red group. "It isn't how you play the game, it's whether you win or lose." Planners, on the other hand, like to win but it is the process that is more important to them.

Are Producers self-confident or arrogant? Most are self-confident. Some take this wonderful attribute too far, and it becomes a limitation. Producers' traits are so strong we often don't know when they slipped over the edge to limitations. These strong personality traits can make it difficult for others to become close to Producers. They know who they are, and they know where they are going. For some of the less-driven personality types, producers look cold, calculating, and even arrogant. Often they are not. They are just being Powerful Producers. However, the stark contrast between this personality type and the other types makes some feel inadequate and insecure.

Producers can also be perceived as bossy, aggressive, intolerant, and controlling. In their quest to produce results, they can manifest these behaviors. They can be hard on people, but they are more often hard on themselves. They can be their own worst critics. They overcome obstacles in order to complete their goals while pushing themselves to do more and more. While the Planners can never get it right, the Producers can never achieve enough.

Powerful Producers are not tolerant of incompetence in anyone. They decide how it should be and move forward. There is a bumper sticker that this red group must have started. It reads, "Be Alert, We Need More Lerts." They are alert, effective, and efficient, and they would appreciate it if everyone would be also.

These kids enjoy having multiple tasks and interests. They sign up for everything from teams to chairmanships of the committees. Remember, they are driven to lead and achieve. Being busy is very important to this group. The term over-achiever is custom-made for this group. For this talented, driven group it may not look like over-achieving, but to the rest of the personality types their commitment level seems over the top.

In our son Matt's senior year in high school, I was certain he was going to crash and burn. He left for water polo practice at 6:00 a.m., working out with weights afterwards. Then he went on to school where he was getting top grades. After school he had some meeting or other because he was always involved with a project to make a difference in something. If his group of friend were having any kind of a social event from proms to ski trips, he would be organizing that also. And, of course, there was the part-time job, the girlfriend, and a few family functions. Most of the time he handled his life platter heaped with commitments with skill and confidence.

Adults Need to Understand This About Powerful Producers:

We Like to Be in Charge of Our Lives. We Want to Do It Our Way and Get Things Done.

For Emotional Growth We Need:
- Respect for the results we have achieved
- Credit for our talents and abilities
- To do it ourselves
- To be right
- Approval for the accomplishments
- Trust that we can do it because we have done other things well

Our Specialties:
- Leadership
- Take charge quickly in an emergency

- Make quick decisions
- Ability to plan ahead
- Make things happen
- Get results
- Trust ourselves more than others
- Ingenious

What Makes Us Mad:

- People who do it wrong or slowly
- Doing something for someone who does it wrong
- Teachers who don't know what they are doing
- Lazy people
- When things are out of control and people won't let us take control
- Coaches who aren't good at coaching

Fears:

- Not doing well in school
- Not winning games and competitions at school
- Looking dumb or stupid
- Not being right
- Nobody cooperating with us
- Being bossed around

What's Fun for Us:

- Winning
- Being in charge
- Going to a special place with friends
- Big family events where we go out of town
- Having an important project and getting it done
- Competition

Help Us with:

- Learning to be compassionate
- Treating others with TLC
- Valuing people for who they are—not what they can do for us

- Being non-judgmental
- Not needing to always be in control
- Not needing to always be right
- Skepticism
- Sarcasm

Attention Grown-ups: This Is Important Stuff!

Needs
To Be Right

Parent Warning: Don't tell these children it can't be done if you don't want to wave a red flag in front of them. Most Producers will take on the challenge just to prove you wrong. They like to be right!

We called our son Matt, Walking Webster, when he was young. He had an opinion on everything, and no one could convince him to the contrary once he decided what was right. Even when he was completely wrong, he almost won people over because he spoke with such confidence and authority.

Dr. James Dobson authored a book titled *The Strong-Willed Child*. If you are the parent of a Powerful Producer, go immediately to your nearest bookstore and get the book. Then read it! The children in the red group can be opinionated and controlling. They want to do everything their way. They want to "do it themselves." From dressing themselves to pouring their own milk, these children are independent and determined to do it their way, which of course is the right way—the only way—their way.

Control

Dana, mother of Daniel, a strong Producer said to me one day in the park, "Watch Daniel." When all the other children his age were perfecting patty-cake and waving bye-bye, Daniel was working on snapping his fingers, pointing at a person, and then motioning him to come to him!

Being born leaders these children know when to take charge. They often don't know how. Instead of diplomacy and collaboration, Producers are often bossy and controlling. My husband and I presently have a red five-year-old in our life. I love to get to school early for pick-up and watch and listen to him on the playground. He is definitely the leader of the pack. He's quite bossy. I notice some of the other kids seem to accept it and take it in stride while others complain to the teacher. One day when I picked him up, the teacher said he'd been controlling all day. With a chuckle she said, "About 11:00 a.m. I thought he might stage a mutiny and take the over class."

If some Producers see a chink in your armor, they may charge. You have to be strong and get in the face of Producers sometimes. The saying "Because I'm the mom, that's why," comes in handy with these children. They understand authority and want to have it in their lives even though they are often challenging you at each step for control.

Opportunities to Move Ahead of the Crowd

These are not children you can expect to march in the middle. They don't have a middle mentality. Give then opportunities to succeed. Most of them are up for the challenge, if it is something that interests them. However, if they are not interested, the saying "you can drag a horse to water but you can't make him drink" applies to parents trying to push or drag these children to do things that don't interest them. Let them pick their interests as long as they are appropriate, then stand back and enjoy the success. Powerful Producers aren't usually too good at stopping to smell the roses. Plant them, grow them, and sell them, but the simple pleasure of enjoying them isn't always easy for Producers.

Producers are generally self-confident. They are sure of what they can achieve. They are not always as sure of who they are as what they can do. Because doing is so important, they don't stop along the way and learn what being is all about. For this red group, being a great "human doing" is easy. Sometimes they have to work on developing relationships, people skills, and compassion to improve their human being part.

Recently, one of the students in my University of California, Irvine class, Producer John, said, "You're right about this people skill thing. Mine are barely decent." Then he laughed and said, "I know I need to work on mine, but I'm too busy accomplishing."

You may need to help your children develop good self-esteem. As self-confident as Producers are, they don't always enjoy good self-esteem. Self-esteem is about loving yourself because you breathe. To Producers breathing isn't much of an accomplishment. It seems everyone is doing that. They need to *do* things that set themselves apart. Help your Powerful Producer child learn the importance of being a good person and loving himself or herself for that goodness.

Taylor is the seven-year-old Powerful Producer granddaughter of my friend Kaye. One of her favorite activities at Grams house is to pretend. Taylor always decides the setting and casts the characters. If it's a castle, Taylor is queen. Grams is always relegated to some servant role. If it's an emergency room, Taylor is the Doctor. Grams is the dying patient. One day Kaye said, "Taylor, today at pretend how about I choose what we play and who plays what?"

Taylor reflected on this a while and said, "O.K. but I get to be the important one."

Producers have strong leadership characteristics. Help them develop appropriate ways to move ahead of the crowd.

The best expression I've heard lately was from a Promoter Mom. She has not one but two Producer children with a Peacekeeper in the middle. She said when she and the Peacekeeper would see the two Producers coming they would turn to one another and say, "Red alert, red alert!"

Good News	Bad News
Independent	Aloof—not often a warm cuddly child
Resourceful	Watch your belongings—they take what they need to make something happen
Logical	Will argue until they wear you down
Determined	Bull-headed
Decisive	Opinionated
Witty	Sarcastic
Positive	All hot air
Global—Big Picture	Head in the clouds—unrealistic

Teenage Producer

Good News	Bad News
Respected	Holds peers at arms length
High Profile	Selfish
Accomplished	Uses people to get where they need to be
Self-assured	Pompous—covering self-doubt
Dynamic	Callous—cold
Driven	Calculating
Forceful	No people skills
Competitive	Do what it takes to win— win at all cost
Capable	Takes on too much
A type	Intense
Inventive	Ruthless
Competent	Intolerant
Leader	Controlling
Take charge	Challenge authority

It looks like no one's in charge —
I'm taking over!

Can't we all be nice to
each other?

CHAPTER 8

Patient Peacekeepers

Patient Peacekeeper • Green • Oval

My neighbors, Robert and Ellen, gave a clear picture of a Peacekeeper child when they talked about their daughter, Emily, who is definitely a Patient Peacekeeper. Ellen said Emily was a caretaker from the moment she was mobile. She was always tender with animals, other babies, children, and her toys. Once school-age, Emily was the friend of the underdog. Not wanting anyone to be excluded or left out, Emily turned their home into a haven for the lost and needy. According to her father, in her teen years she added the weird. Thanks to Emily and her kind heart, one of her projects stayed in their home a week and gave everyone head lice.

Robert recalls the time she brought home a litter of newborn kittens abandoned by their mother. For this act of love the whole family got ringworm. Robert shrugged his shoulders and said, "Emily's so kind and caring with the purest of motives. We couldn't get angry at her—even when we got ringworm. I have to be careful not to tell Emily I'm disappointed in her. It destroys her. She is the most compassionate and sensitive member of our family. In fact, sometimes she puts the rest of the family to shame because she really is her brother/sister's keeper, and the rest of us are busy focusing on ourselves. Emily is a gentle, tender-heart who really loves and cares about people."

I have watched Emily from birth to womanhood. She is a bright girl who approached school like she does life. She took school slowly and steadily, trying not to get stressed out anymore than absolutely necessary. She got the grades she needed to go to college. She went to the college of her choice, graduated with good enough grades to get into the master's program of her choice, and worked as a corporate psychologist in a large company. Emily knows who she is and what she needs, more than any young person I know.

One Christmas break she told me she was taking a semester off. She said, "I broke my own rules last semester. I tried to work and take too many classes. I got a huge case of the 'whelms.'"

Of course, I asked her to define "whelms."

She said, "I've always known I couldn't load my plate as much as Tim, my A-type driven brother. He likes life in the fast lane, taking on more that three people can handle. I don't. I like to take life steadily and practically. I like space and independence with little outside demands on me. It's important for me to keep my life manageable. Otherwise I get overwhelmed quickly. A bad case of overwhelmed becomes the 'whelms.' When I'm 'whelmed,' the peace and harmony I must have goes away, and I become passive resistive and apathetic. I drop out emotionally. I become too overwhelmed to function. That's where I am right now. So, I'm going to get off the merry-go-round, regroup, and try again in summer school."

Now, I'm watching Emily function in her role as wife and mother. I had coffee with Emily recently and listened to the update on her life. She said, "I don't like juggling too many balls at a time. I knew I did not want to be a working mother. So we sacrifice because I don't work, but it's worth it. I keep my life as peaceful and steady as I can, considering I have three young children. I've started a Mothers of Pre-Schools (MOPS) group. Being a stay-at-home mom can be lonely and isolating, and I would hate to think of other women in that place when there is companionship and support out there. Organizing this group is enough for me right now. I'm learning to set good boundaries because I have such a high need to keep everyone happy and everything harmonious. If I didn't have good boundaries, people would walk all over me, and then I'd be an overwhelmed doormat."

As I drove home from my meeting with Emily I was thinking that this kind, considerate, needing to please child has grown into a woman who is gracious, diplomatic, and compassionate.

Plus, she has a good understanding of her own strengths and limitation. How blessed her family is.

Adults need to understand about Patient Peacekeepers:

We Like a Life That Is as Conflict Free as Possible.

For Emotional Growth We Need:
- To have you understand our personality type
- To be accepted for who we are not what we do
- To have you help us feel we have worth
- To have you understand we have kind hearts
- Respect
- Independence

Our Specialties:
- Balance
- Diplomacy
- Calm, cool, collected
- Kind, nice, and easy to get along with
- Adaptable
- Being practical and having common sense
- Being pleasant
- Concerned with how others feel
- Cooperative

What Makes Us Sad:
- When people are angry
- People fighting
- Mean people
- When no one helps us with mean people
- When we are blamed for something we didn't do
- Being ignored
- People being left out

Fears:
- Things changing all the time
- Not being considered good people
- Too many things to do at once
- Problems
- Dealing with problems

What Is Enjoyable for Us:
- Family outings when everyone gets along
- Friends and family over when everyone gets along
- Working on something we like either alone or with a friend
- Parties where no one is left out
- School when everyone is nice
- Sometimes teams—but with a coach that doesn't shout or exclude players

Help Us with:
- Speaking up for ourselves
- Being too sensitive
- Being taken advantage of by more dominating people
- Joining in what is going on around us
- Not getting lost in the shuffle
- Being too kind and nice

Attention Grown-ups: This Is Important Stuff!

Needs
Status Quo

Peacekeepers don't want their boats of life rocking, tipping from side to side, and definitely not capsizing. They don't want to radically change courses either. They want to plot a slow but steady course and sail along in the tranquil waters of life. When their boat of life is sailing along smoothly, it gives them time to experience the peace and harmony that they believe life is suppose to have.

Divorce or separation for these children violates this high need for status quo. These children usually don't act out; they withdraw. When, and if, they act out, it will come with a force that has a great deal of stored up emotion behind it.

After I discussed the Peacekeeper child in one seminar, a mother told me this story.

"I have two children, Zach, a Producer who's fourteen, and Kevin, a Peacekeeper who's twelve. I have been divorced for two years. The first year Zach verbally bombarded me with accusations, criticisms, assertions, and an opinion about exactly how I should handle everything. Life with him was like living with a verbal machine gun— a constant ratta tat tat of words piercing my soul. Zach was brutal.

Kevin, who had always been a quiet, compliant child, became almost stoic. I knew it was not a good sign. Between my personal pain of having my husband leave me for another woman and my Producer son never shutting up, I pretty much let Kevin quietly drift that first year.

Zach was always huffing and puffing, like a strong, constant annoying wind of words. But Kevin was like a tornado, calm, until it blew through wiping everything out. One day in year two, Kevin blew. In one week he kicked a teacher's aide, ripped all the flowers out of my garden, and ran away from home for twenty-four hours before we found him.

At the end of the week the three of us started therapy. Kevin is learning how to express himself in appropriate ways, a little at a time, instead of keeping it in, then blowing. Zach is learning to be a little more compassionate and less judgmental and opinionated. I'm learning more about all three of us so we can meet each other's needs and start to enjoy life again.

I am a Promoter desperately wanting some fun to return to our lives."

Independence

Peacekeepers can be very outgoing and social and also extremely content in solitary activities. These children report that they like to read, build models, do puzzles, and play with Legos™. They also enjoy arts and crafts and computers.They enjoy a variety of quiet activities. For most of this green group, spending time alone in pursuit of something they enjoy is a very good thing.

Having friends and being a friend is very important, but these children can also stand apart from the crowd and be their own person. They know who they are, and most know what they want. Compliant by nature, Peacekeepers can be pushed only so far. When they take their independent stand it might look like stubbornness with a silent will of iron.

Comfort

Of all the personality types, these Peacekeeper children have the highest need for comfort. Comfort in all forms—from their clothing to their food to their environment. If your green child is having a bad day, remember you can comfort this child with favorite, familiar foods. This child will also respond positively to an ordered, quiet setting. Perhaps giving your child a backrub while he/she tells you about the upsets of the day will be just what this peaceful child needs to find balance again.

My friend, Susan, has a Peacekeeper son, Will. As a nursing infant Will would reach for his mother's long hair and rub it on his face while feeding. Susan learned that Will wanted soft sheets and blankets in his crib and later on his bed. He would, again, gently rub the fabric on his face as he went to sleep. When Will was distressed, Susan would often find him in his room reading or listening to music but always with a soft blanket close at hand to rub. The ability to comfort themselves is a skill these green group children often learn early in life.

Good News	Bad News
Compliant	Passive-resistive
Diplomatic	Wishy-washy
Listens	Stoic
Kind	Smothering
Supportive	Uninvolved
Calm	Unenthusiastic
Steady	Overwhelmed
Patient	Indecisive
Malleable	Stubborn

Teenage Peacekeeper

Good News	Bad News
Concerned	Co-dependent
Creative dressers	Weird
Independent	Isolated – loner
Nonchalant	Lazy
Accomodating	Used by peers
Compassionate	Non-assertive
Slow-paced	Unmotivated
Individualists	Non-conforming
Caring	Apathetic
Balanced	Cannot be motivated by what others think

Parent Alert

The Peacekeeper child in the classroom is sometimes invisible. They quietly sit, steadily doing the work, trying to fit in so they don't draw attention to themselves. They don't make waves or get in trouble, and they definitely don't do anything to upset the teacher. In this present day with chaos in many classrooms, green group kids can be a joy, but they are often overlooked and slip through the cracks. *Parents, talk to the teachers to make sure they know your child is there and getting his or her needs met.*

Hey, what's the rush?

SECTION THREE

More or Less Alike?

SECTION THREE

More or Less Alike?

Similarities and Differences
Between the Four Personality Types

I n this section I will compare and contrast the different personality types with each other. My seminar participants, when surveyed or interviewed, shared that the children who have their personality type and closest personality color shade are the children they understand the best. It is these children with whom they feel they are connecting and succeeding. The ones they don't understand are the children who have the complete opposite personality from the adult. These are the children they must come to understand in order to connect with them, meet their needs, and love them.

We all have opposite personality types. Promoters and Planners are opposite while Peacekeepers and Producers are opposite.

The number one question I am asked as I travel around the country speaking about personality types is, "Do opposites attract when it comes to mates?" My answer comes from four sources—statistical data, audience feedback, observation, and my own marriage. My answer is, "Absolutely, opposites attract for dating and marriage. We are attracted to that which we least understand. We marry them and spend the rest of our lives succeeding or failing at understanding them. We are frustrated because they are not like us. Yet, isn't that exactly what attracted us in the first place?"

CHAPTER 9

Similarities and Differences

Although the focus of this book is to understand the children in our lives, I want to briefly address the dynamic between two personality types when they marry and become parents. Yes, opposites attract. The two most common marriages I see and hear about are the blue Planner married to the yellow Promoter and that of the red Producer married to the green Peacekeeper.

On the next pages you will find a "Similarities and Differences" chart for all the personality types. The first chart is the Promoter/Planner comparison. If you will notice, there are two similarities and seventeen differences. If you are in this kind of a marriage or relationship, a look at the chart should make you laugh or cry, depending on how you are managing the differences.

The stories I hear from this personality type combination are all different, but the topic is the same. This personality partnership disagrees and/or fights (depending on the maturity level and emotional healthiness of the couple) over systems and order. The Planners want systems and order in everything, and the Promoters are racing through life with no time to get a plan much less bring order to it. Although Promoters enjoy the freedom of their style, this unstructured and inventive lifestyle sometimes drives their Planner spouses crazy.

Planner Carla, married to Promoter Dwayne successfully for over twenty-five years, gave this advice to other Planners who are also married to Promoters:

- Don't give them the original of anything.
- Keep separate checking accounts unless you like yours in a mess and often overdrawn.
- If the event begins at 7:00 p.m. tell them 6:30 p.m. so you will only be five minutes late.
- Always carry your own airplane ticket.
- Don't get your feelings hurt because your mate is the fun one and you are seen as the sensible one.
- Keep a positive attitude when your mate comes up with another new idea and you have to implement it.
- Remember you married him or her because he or she was so casual and social.

Promoter Dwayne's advice on how to live with a Planner:

- Buy her or him a tee shirt that says, "Go with the Flow."
- Understand that she or he is going for getting it right— the spouse might seem critical.
- Ignore the nit-picky times.
- Know that she or he is practical.
- Understand when she or he does not like change.
- Enjoy the fact that she or he pays attention to details, then you don't have to.
- Respect her or him for being so dependable.
- Remember you were attracted to this serious, no-nonsense person.

Planners that complain about their Promoter spouses all seem to sound like this. "I was attracted to the energy, charm, and strong social skills. Now I want him to stop talking to his friends, calm down, and get organized." Meanwhile Promoters complain that his or her original attraction to this serious, down to earth, analytical spouse has turned to boredom and confinement. The Planner constantly needs to be cheered up and encouraged by the Promoter while making the Promoter spouse feel inferior, inadequate, and sometimes stupid.

As you study the Similarity and Differences chart for Producers and Peacekeepers you will find two similarities and eighteen differences. The similarities are Logic and Independence. The Producers are logic-based thinkers. The Peacekeepers are emotionally or feelings-based, but they are logical. However, because Producers process everything through their brains while the Peacekeepers process through their hearts first—the logic is very different.

A classic argument of these couples is over facts verses feelings. The Producer states, "The facts speak for themselves." The Peacekeeper argues for feelings to be included. Many Producers, by their own admissions, have trouble getting into feelings and emotions.

Dave, a Producer, is successful in business but just divorced his fifth wife. After a seminar he said, "I had decided I should stay in the logical world of business where I fit and quit trying to find my heart. I think it's buried under too many *Wall Street Journals*. But after today, like the Tin Man in the Wizard of Oz, I guess I'll go in search of my heart. You've made it sound like the thing to do."

The second thing that the Producer/Peacekeeper marriage has in common is independence. However, this commonality is the source of much disagreement for this couple. Peacekeepers love independence for themselves and everyone else. They don't want to control or be controlled. So, of course, they marry the most controlling personality, the Producer. Producers want complete independence for themselves. No one is going to tell them what to do! But they are often very controlling with others. So these two personality types like independence, but they view it from different perspectives and disagree over it.

Producers are often attracted to the gentleness and quiet spirits of their spouses. However, they also knew, at some level, they could control their mates. After living with them awhile, Producers want Peacekeepers to get more enthusiastic and excited about what is going on in their lives and quit being doormats.

Peacekeepers are often attracted to power and decisiveness in their Producer spouses. Later they feel this Producer spouse has become controlling and dominating and grow tired of being pushed around.

Different or opposite personality types are the ones that challenge us. It is these differences in personalities that make us wish we had "Do Over Coupons." In this next section, you will find two different types of charts that will help you learn more about you and the children in your life. These are the guides for "training up children the way they should go." Guiding a child with insight and understanding is the loving way.

Similarities and Differences

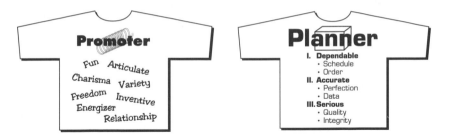

Similarities

People interaction is important
Acceptance and approval from others is of utmost importance

Differences

PROMOTER	PLANNER
• Simple personality	• Complex personality
• Playful and casual	• Serious and formal
• High profile	• Low profile
• Large groups	• Intimate groups
• Trusting	• Suspicious
• Innovative	• Creative
• Flexible	• Structured
• Spontaneous	• Planned
• Likes change	• Dislikes change
• Scattered productivity	• Systematic productivity
• Hang loose	• Uptight
• Direct	• Indirect
• Close enough	• Precise
• Generalist	• Specialist
• Possibilities	• Practical
• Relationships	• Tasks
• Feeling	• Thinking

Similarities and Differences

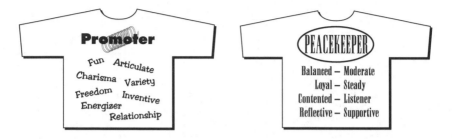

Similarities

Relationship oriented • Casual style • Good natured
Patient • Welcome advice • Tolerant • Accepting
Forgiving • Non-judgmental • Feeling

Differences

PROMOTER	PEACEKEEPER
• Spontaneous	• Steady
• High profile	• Low profile
• Possibilities	• Practical
• Stimulating	• Soothing
• Aggressive	• Passive
• Pro-active	• Reactive
• Impulsive	• Methodical
• Emotional	• Logical
• Socialite	• Loner
• Likes change	• Dislike change

Similarities and Differences

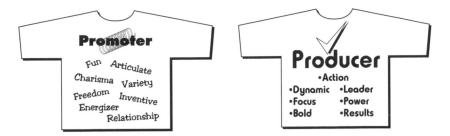

Similarities

Strong verbal skills • Loves freedom • Risk takers
Arguments stimulate them • Rebellious • Non-conforming
Possibility oriented • Present and future oriented
Innovative • Inventive • Entrepreneurial

Differences

PROMOTER	PRODUCER
• Relationship oriented	• Task oriented
• Good natured	• Impatient
• Carefree	• Intense
• Non-possessive	• Possessive
• Scattered productivity	• Targeted productivity
• Accepts advice	• Does not want advice
• Unfocused	• Driven
• Undisciplined	• Well disciplined
• Shares emotions	• Does not share emotions
• Feeling	• Thinking

Similarities and Differences

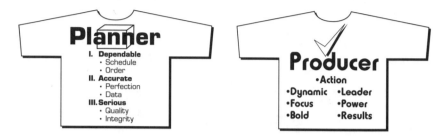

Similarities

Achievers • Want to be in control
Task oriented • Determined • Responsible
Makes decision with head • Complex personalities

Differences

PLANNER

- Detailed
- Specifics
- Dislikes change
- Self-righteous
- Pessimistic
- Focuses on past
- Practical
- Perfectionist
- Indirect
- Process
- Quality
- Analytical

PRODUCER

- General
- Big picture
- Creates change
- Arrogant
- Optimistic
- Focuses on future
- Possibilities
- Productivity
- Direct
- Progress
- Quantity
- Logical

Similarities and Differences

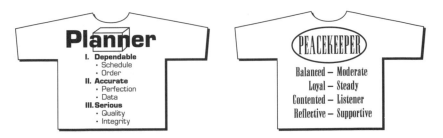

Similarities

Practical • Steady
Compliant with rules • Dislikes change

Differences

PLANNER	PEACEKEEPER
• Task oriented	• Relationship oriented
• To be good morally	• To feel good within
• Analytical	• Logical
• Intense	• Relaxed
• Focuses on past	• Focused on present
• Demanding	• Non-demanding
• Complex personality	• Simple personality
• Formal	• Casual
• Thinking	• Feeling
• Highly structured	• Medium to low structure
• Self-focused	• Other focused
• Self-righteous	• Non-judgemental
• Needs to belong and affiliate	• Self contained
• Likes group process	• Solo or very small group
• Leadership	• Independence

Similarities and Differences

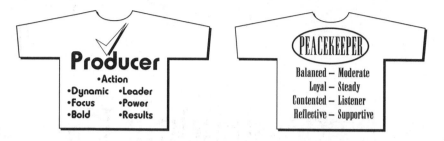

Similarities

Logical
Independent

Differences

PRODUCER	PEACEKEEPER
• Task oriented	• Relationship oriented
• Control others	• Control self
• Please self	• Please others
• Change	• Stability
• Delegator	• Doer
• Tense	• Relaxed
• Impatient	• Patient
• Demanding	• Non-demanding
• Tactless	• Tactful
• Gives Advice	• Seeks advice
• Poor listener	• Good listener
• Possibilities	• Practical
• Thinking	• Feeling
• Multi-tasking	• Single projects
• Likes lots to do	• Overwhelmed with too much
• Achievement	• Enjoying
• Doing	• Being
• Results	• Process

CHAPTER 10

Understanding Us

Profile of Promoter Parents and Other Promoter Adults with:

Perky Promoter Children
Precise Planner Children
Powerful Producer Children
Patient Peacekeeper Children

Living life to the fullest and having fun while you're at it is important to Promoters. Many Promoters are just grown-up kids, so they are great at playing with their children. This relationship-oriented group enjoys big people and little people, socializing, and freedom. Energetic and spontaneous, these parents are usually involved in a variety of activities and events with their children. Life with a Promoter parent is anything but routine and boring.

Born encouragers and motivators, Promoter parents often serve as personal cheerleaders to their children and any other child who crosses their path. Most in this yellow group express a real love for children.

Some Promoter parents need to work on structure and follow through in the lives of their children. A fun-filled high adventure life may be good for the parent but not always the child.

Perky Promoters

There usually is not lack of love in this relationship. Both are good at self-expression so communication is generally OK to great.

Lack of structure, no attention to details, and forgetfulness can plague this relationship. The Promoter adult will need to model materials and time management to these hang-loose kids. These children have creative minds flooded with an idea per minute. Organizing everything from thoughts to belongings and schoolwork can be challenging. Since both adults and children like a great deal of variety, focusing should be worked on in this relationship.

Managing relationships is usually easy for these children. Due to their "go for the gusto" attitude and love for people and life, they are usually popular with peers. Telephones ringing and friends coming and going are not uncommon if you have Promoter children.

The adult Promoters should understand the social nature of Perky Promoters.

Precise Planners

This parent child relationship has less in common than more in common. These children want routines, structure, and order. These traits do not come naturally to most Promoters. Planner children like to be on time and follow a schedule. Late adults are upsetting to these children. Disorganization and unscheduled changes are difficult for these orderly kids to manage. Planner children want to get life right. Details and quality are important to them.

Planner children can be rather serious and no nonsense. Promoters are playful and casual. Help the Planner children in your life to find the light side of life. Some Promoter adults need to get their acts together in order to be more effective in the lives of Planner children.

Powerful Producers

The shared traits of parents and children are in their enjoyment of adventure and some element of risk. Both are innovative possibility thinkers with strong verbal skills. Promoter parents love freedom and so do their Producer children. These parents need to give these children as much freedom as is reasonable and safe. In most cases these independent, determined, responsible children can handle appropriate responsibilities. Over advising and controlling will not work with these "I've got it together, get out of my way," children.

It is possible that these children may be more determined about the events of their lives than the parents. Producer children want to take on life in a big way. Leadership traits may show up early in these children. The flip side of being a strong dynamic leader is manipulation, domination, and over-controlling. Promoter parents have good people skills and should model win/win leadership for these bold children.

Patient Peacekeepers

The commonality between these parents and children is their tender-hearts and relationship skills. Both care about people and want to please others. Promoter parents with their high need for variety, action, and activities in their lives can overwhelm these slower-paced children. A word of advice to parents—give these green group children advance notice of changes in plans and schedules when possible. They need some processing time to adjust to change. Everyone will be happier if these children do not have to change courses abruptly.

These children are often contented, self-contained, and do not need life to be a three-ring circus. Most of these children prefer to take life in small steady steps, not quantum leaps.

Peacekeeper children are generally not as social as Promoters are. One or two quality friends are comfortable for them. They do not need a cast of thousands running in and out of their lives. Many relationships to manage can bring confusion and chaos to these keep-life-simple-and-calm children.

Peacekeeper children have a high need to please. Encouragement and affirmations go a long way with these children. Remember these children are about peace. Anger, rage, and ugliness make these children retreat inside themselves to avoid life when it is not about peace and harmony.

Profile of Planner Parents and Other Planner Adults with:

Precise Planner Children
Perky Promoter Children
Powerful Producer Children
Patient Peacekeeper Children

Traditional values of family, education, and often religion are important to this group. Most Planners are concerned with providing stability, security, and routine for their children. The Planners need for an orderly life filters down into their parenting.

Planners want their children to achieve *but* to achieve the right way. Process is very important for this personality type. These analytical, practical parents have plenty of suggestions for the right way to do things. Many parents in this group like to tell their children not only what to do but also how to do it.

Some are very narrow in their view of the right way. They place perfectionist, unreal expectations on their children. Many Planner parents are guilt-ridden because of their eternal quest to get everything right and, of course, life is not perfect, so they experience some sense of failure and guilt. Planner parents often pass guilt down to their children. Some parents do it knowingly and others unknowingly.

Their Planner children can absorb this guilt because they, too, are plagued with trying to do life perfectly, and guilt can find a home in some of these children. The Promoter or Producer children who have Planner parents aren't as likely to absorb the guilt as their Planner siblings might.

Precise Planners

The Planner parent can help Planner children establish systems and order in their lives. These children are trying to get things in life done right. Help them do it right. Some Planner children have perfectionistic tendencies. Do what you can as a parent to help them target and hit realistic goals. Even Planner parents with Planner children might find these children are more perfectionistic than their parents or vice versa. This can be a source of frustration.

Modeling options and alternate solutions to these children is important. Precise Planners take life seriously. As the adult you are responsible to bring lightness and encouragement to these no nonsense children.

Perky Promoters

These free spirit children do not care about systems and order because systems and order look like boundaries and containment. Many Promoter children are not good at managing materials and belongings. Something they own is always lost or missing. Many in this group are just plain messy.

The Planner parents and Promoter children are opposite in most ways. The Planner parent is task-oriented trying to get life right while the Promoter child is relationship-oriented wanting to live life and have fun.

Some Planner parents have an inflexible nature. Rigidity and details will not work with most Promoter children. Do not try to capture or contain these children with rigid rules and restrictive structure. They will spend all their time and energy trying to figure out how to get the freedom they want and need. The harder you squeeze the more they will struggle to get free. Eventually this struggle will turn into rebellion.

These are possibility-thinking children with high energy. You want to work with them toward managing their own lives with as much freedom as is reasonably safe to give them. They have a playful nature, and you need to make the playgrounds of their lives safe but large enough that they can experience life in their expansive way.

The problem here is many of these children don't look like they have their acts together. Remember these are children who do not want their acts together—especially by Planner parent standards. They like winging it through life. Life must be an exciting adventure, and if you have parents with a detailed map, then where is the thrill?

Planner parents with their schedules and plans may become frustrated with these children. Remember these children are not like you, and their ways are *not* your ways. Motivating and encouraging with tons of verbal affirmations versus rigid rules and severe punishments works better with these children. As hard as it going to be for you, the more space you can realistically give these social, energetic children—the more they will find their own flexible boundaries. These children will profit from logical consequences of stepping outside the boundaries you have set rather than from punishment. (See Chapter 12 under Threats)

Powerful Producers

These children are probably going to have a larger worldview and be more visionary than you are. They will achieve and accomplish but may be aiming for quantity first and quality later—if ever. You may frustrate them by giving too many specifics and details. These are big picture children who like to lead and be in charge. Control can be an issue here. Planner parents need to guard against being nit-picky and appreciate that these children have a vision of the big picture not the details that make up that picture.

These results oriented children believe in doing what it takes to get the job done–the end justifies the means. Coaching and guiding these children usually works better than rigid rules and tight controls.

Patient Peacekeepers

Planner parents will provide the stable systems and routine these green group children need. Warning to Planners: Some of these children will give "slow-paced" new meaning. Allow time in your daily schedule for these children who sometimes move at a tortoise's pace because that's the pace they like. These are children who have no need to rush through life—strolling suits them perfectly. Giving your Peacekeeper children space and their own pace will eliminate lots of nagging and frustration for both of you.

Some Peacekeeper children can be stubborn and passive resistive. The more you nag, the deeper they dig in their heals, and neither of you is happy. As you respect their need for independence and pace, you will find these children more malleable and less stubborn.

Peacekeeper children are little tender-hearts who want right relationships. Tension and lack of harmony are hard on these children. Help them move through life with as much steadiness and balance as possible.

Note: Regarding divorce and separations. Remembering that steadiness and predictability are key for Planner and Peacekeeper children, divorce is going to be particularly hard on these children. Divorce brings change. Divorce brings instability and disharmony. Peacekeeper children, who are going through life looking for relationships that work, are going to be particularly hard hit by any kind of domestic discord.

Profile of Producer Parents and Other Producer Adults with:

Powerful Producer Children
Precise Planner Children
Perky Promoter Children
Patient Peacekeeper Children

Winning at the game of life is extremely important to Producers. Most Producer parents put pressure, seen and unseen, on their children to get their acts together, accomplish, and win. This attitude applies to school, sports, after school activities, and work. Many Producers are what has become popularly referred to as "Type-A" personalities. They are driven to be competent and successful.

This group tries to pass their attitudes and drive onto their children. Some of their Producer and Planner children will resonate with their task-oriented, driven parents. But often their Promoter and Peacekeeper children aren't running life as a race with goals and winning in mind. They are living life for the sheer joy of just experiencing it — win, lose, or draw. Producer parents need to realize not every person is as competitive, determined, and goal-oriented as they are.

Being task-oriented, Producer parents need to remember that raising a child is more about relationship than a task. Too many people in this red group focus on the tasks involved with a child and forget to relate. Hugging and laughter might be valid goals for this week!

Most Producer parents could lighten-up a little—or a lot—depending on the personalities of their children.

Powerful Producers

This is a battle of the wills. Both are strong. These children were born with a need to be in charge of life. Parents need to find ways to let these children earn independence and freedom. Remember these children value what you value—accomplishment, competency, and winning. Help them learn appropriate skills and attitudes to find achievement.

Producer children usually need guidelines and coaching, not rigidity and tight controls. Most Producer children are self-starters and need you by their side without pulling or pushing. Many of these children will put plenty of pressure on themselves—more from you may be too much!

Precise Planners

These children want to achieve and accomplish just as you do. The difference is Producer Parents often insist on telling the child what and how to achieve. Planners are masters at figuring out systems and procedures. Generally, these children are going to be more perfectionist than their parents. Planner children want to accomplish with quality while their Producer parents are more concerned about quantity.

Parents need to set the guidelines for the "whats" of their children's lives, but if they could give these children some latitude in the "hows" these children would probably do very well. In most cases they will find their children know how to do what the parents want.

Parents need to find ways to let these children earn independence and freedom with the structures and processes of their lives.

Perky Promoters

Most Promoter children are not as results-oriented as their Producer parents. These children are free spirited. Do not try to capture or contain them in a too small space. They will spend all their time and energy trying to figure out how to get the freedom they want and need.

These are possibilities-oriented children with high energy. You want to work with them not against them. They are playful by nature, and you need to make the playgrounds of their lives safe but large enough for them to do some discovering on their own.

Some Producers have a controlling nature. Rigidity and domination will not work with these Promoter children. The harder you squeeze, the more they will struggle to get free. Eventually this struggle will turn into rebellion.

The problem here is many of these children don't look like they have their act together. Remember that these children don't want their act together—especially by Producer parent standards. They like winging it through life. Life must be an exciting adventure. The thrill of the hunt is important to them. Producer adults are focusing on completion and winning. These children's main focus is the event itself. Finish would be good, winning would be good, also, but the process and the happening is the real thrill. Being there and making new friends along the way are important to Promoter children.

Producer parents and Producer adults, with their goals and targeted plans, may frustrate these children. Remember these children are not like you, and their ways are *not* your ways. You will need to give many more verbal affirmations to these children than you think they've earned. Encouraging these children is *not* about their earning it–it is about their needing it. You need to stand beside them as a cheerleader with tons of "U can do and U are great" cheers.

Patient Peacekeepers

These children are of a very different nature than their Producer parents and other Producer adults. These children are peacemakers and peacekeepers. They will go far out of their way to avoid conflicts and scenes. Family discord is extremely hard on these children. They are kind, gentle children. Peacekeepers may or may not be driven to accomplish, but if there is a drive for something, they will quietly and independently go after what they want. This parent/child combination has different action styles.

Control is an issue. These children want a life that is independent. They don't want to control anyone and resent being controlled by others. Guidance that is fair and appropriate they understand and accept. They want their space and do not like confrontation, domination, or forcefulness. These children will say "Yes" to keep the peace but will often not do what they said they would do. They can be stubborn and passive resistive.

Peacekeepers are compliant. They lead life with their hearts and can be gentle—but do not mistake this for weakness. They have a silent will of iron, which you do not want to have to confront. Understand and work with them. Do not try to control them.

Producer parents need to understand and respect these children for who they are and how different they are from themselves. Most of these children do better with softer parenting skills. These children want to please and avoid conflict. Don't push them. Rather take their hands and walk beside them with gentleness. Give these green children advance notice of changes in plans and schedule when possible. They need some processing time to adjust to change. Everyone will be happier if this child does not have to change courses abruptly.

This child may not ever want to achieve in the way you do. Being a good human being is more important to these children than being a good human "doing"!

Note to Producer Fathers:

If you have a Peacekeeper son, there is a good chance this child is not as competitive as you are. If you are into competitive sports, your son may not be into competitive sports or even individual sports. You may have a son, much to your dismay, who will never want to play football, tennis, or soccer. Your child may be interested in other things. If you have an individualist, try to find something that you both mutually enjoy. Support him in the things that interest him, and you enjoy the things that interest you. Pushing this passive child to be something he is not is destruction in the long term.

Remember the father in my introduction who fell in the swimming pool at his son's swim meet? This was a bright red Producer father with a pale green son. That son has now grown up. He is successful in the computer programming industry. He is a gentle and compassionate father. He never does anything competitively, but his children play soccer because they enjoy it. He lives across the country from his father—by choice. He and his family rarely visit his father.

Profile of Peacekeeper Parents and Other Peacekeeper Adults with:

Patient Peacekeepers
Precise Planners
Powerful Producers
Perky Promoters

These are the parents with heart. This green group brings balance, fairness, and a strong sense of what others are feeling to parenting. Peacekeepers like life to be balanced and calm. However, their "don't-rock-the-boat" motto forgot to include children! Children, by their very nature, bring situations that rock the boat. Most Peacekeepers have the ability to float above the craziness of parenting. They stay calm, cool, and collected come what may.

Peacekeeper parents promote harmony in the family. They are good listeners, using their strong negotiating skills to bring peace to the "did not" and "did too" of sibling rivalry.

They are accepting and sometimes too gentle. These parents err sometimes on the side of leniency. Because they do not like to be forced into activities or behaviors, neither are they comfortable forcing their children into activities and behaviors that the children resist. So an internal struggle for many Peacekeeper parents is knowing how much pushing is productive and when is pushing too much. However, these patient parents can "lay down the law," when they need to.

Patient Peacekeepers

These parents understand these children's nature. They are both low-key and even-tempered. They both try to go through life doing their own thing.

Peacekeeper children want to please. Pleasing looks like keeping the peace. These harmony-driven children are all for a calm, stable environment.

Many children in this green group are self-contained and non-demanding. They are sometimes the kids who slip through the cracks in large groups like classrooms and youth groups. But Peacekeeper parents know this about their children, and most are watching. Peacekeeper adults prefer to ignore conflict situations, but they need to speak up and be advocates for these children.

These children prefer a single project at a time and like to set their own pace and work independently or with a friend. Parents need to help them not to be overwhelmed by the demands of life. Many children in this group are easily overwhelmed with too many demands placed on their time. They like steady, status quo situations with minimal amounts of change. A word of advice to parents—give these green children advance notice of changes in plans and schedules when possible. They need some processing time to adjust to change. Everyone will be happier if these children do not have to change courses abruptly.

These children enjoy being part of a team that is accepting and supporting. Because of their sense of fairness and fair play they may not be highly competitive.

Precise Planners

The similarities this parent/child combination enjoys are their practical outlook on life, a desire for a life that is steady and planned, and compliance with rules.

Some Planner children may want more structure and details in their lives than their parents do. These are children who like routine, schedules, and knowing what's going to happen next.

133

The Peacekeeper parents may have to stretch to provide the systems and order in life that their children need.

Some Planner children may have perfectionist tendencies. Help them set realistic goals for themselves that they can achieve. These children usually want to be good students and get good grades. They manage their time and materials well. The structure of the education process fills these children's need for systems and order. Because of these children's need for predictability they do not like change. Moving, changes to the family, and divorce are very difficult for the children in the blue group.

Powerful Producers

These children have a very different nature than their Peacekeeper parents. While the parents like life in the middle to slow lanes, the kids live in the fast lane. These are strong willed children. Powerful Producers are determined, often demanding, self pleasing, and ready to run the world.

Producer children are born wanting to be in charge of life. Remember, these children value independence as much or more than their Peacekeeper parents. Parents need to find ways to let these children earn independence and freedom. Help them to learn appropriate skills and attitudes to achieve this.

These children usually need guidelines and coaching—not rigidity and tight controls. Most Producer children are self-starters. Frankly, since you are not forceful in your parenting style, let these self-starters go longer and push harder than you would most likely prefer them to. Your supporting nature can compliment their desire to accomplish. Just be careful not to diminish it. Many of these children will put plenty of pressure on themselves to achieve and succeed. Help them to be nice to themselves. Peacekeeper parents, be ready to enjoy a fast bumpy ride!

Help these children learn tenderness toward the human race. They are logic based while you are emotional based. You may need to give special teaching to the areas of people skills and TLC.

Perky Promoters

The parents and these children both make their decisions with their hearts. People, relationships, values, and feelings are commonalties for this combination. They are both people-persons. Friendliness, caring, acceptance, and a good nature are characteristics of both personalities.

The Promoter children want more going on in life than Peacekeepers usually do. These freewheeling, activity-a-minute children do not want a steady, status quo life like their parents. Life with Promoter children can feel busy and chaotic.

Many Promoter children seem to need help with structure, attention to details, and forgetfulness. These children are moving fast down the road of life and have little time for organization. Their creative minds are flooded with an idea a minute. Organizing everything from thoughts to belonging and schoolwork can be challenging for these children. The Peacekeeper parent will need to teach these children time management skills. Peacekeeper parents know how to focus and stick with a project—usually their Promoter children do not. Teach them, but don't do it for them.

These are rock-your-boat children. Due to their "go for the gusto" attitude and love for people and life, these children are often popular. Promoter children enjoy life. These Pied Piper children welcome friends, friends, and more friends. Telephones ringing and friends coming and going are all part of the Promoter children's lives. Peacekeeper adults—just take a motion sickness pill and enjoy the scenery.

Using What You've Learned

SECTION FOUR

Using What
You've Learned

The last section comes from a culmination of my own parenting experience, my conversations and encounters with parents and teachers, and my nonprofit work in advocating for kids. Over the years, I have seen pain and regret in the eyes of adults who want to do a better job and worry that there are no "Do Over" Coupons. For those of us who really do care about the kids in our lives, we just want to understand how to "do better" before it's "too late." Here we will look at practical ways to apply what we've come to understand about ourselves and the kids in our lives.

As you read on, remember that though each child-adult relationship is unique, really knowing *who* your children are will give you a good start on building—or rebuilding—a positive relationship that will help them grow into the people God intended them to be. It may not always be easy—after all, the plans we have for our children seem so good, don't they? But don't give up! You might just be pleasantly surprised to discover that what God intended in designing your children is so much greater than what you had in mind!

CHAPTER 11

The Parenting Kit

L eaving the hospital with our first child, Matthew, we felt a false sense of security. The hospital was sending us home with a Parenting Kit that would meet our son's needs for the first few days — well, his physical needs anyway. We quickly realized meeting the physical needs was the easy part.

The supermarket and drugstore shelves are lined with items to help meet children's physical needs from formula to thermometers. However, let's go to the bookstore shelves and see what's available to help us meet our children's emotional needs. There are some excellent parental advice books, but if you compare shelf space between the physical needs and the emotional needs, you will see that physical needs are winning the shelf-space contest. Early in an infant's life emotional needs quickly come to the forefront of parenting challenges. So, where is that kit anyway?

If the hospital sent us home with a Parenting Kit for Emotional Needs for our child's whole life, what would be in it? The foundation of the kit would be unconditional love, layered with parental maturity. Good character qualities like patience, kindness, goodness, faithfulness, gentleness, and self-control for parents would come next. Throw in a huge amount of wisdom and humor, and we've got a strong start on a great Parenting Kit.

Our unconditional love says, "I love you because you exist." In unconditional love there is no room for measuring performance and achievement. It's not yo-yo love, up and down, depending upon how well the child interacts with others, behaves, or achieves.

Love looks different to different parents. Todd and Lee were both raised in alcoholic homes. To this couple love looked like an absence of substances and a schedule upon which their children could count. Neither parent was mature enough to be emotionally available for their children, but they both were sure they were raising their children in a loving environment. Their children had their physical needs met but were hungry in the love department.

Unconditional love is the foundation, but there needs to be more. Love must be built upon mature parents who understand children's personalities. Mature parents know how to get their own needs met so they can focus on their children's needs.

Remember this is about focus. Parents with immature maturity levels can be ineffective in the parent child relationship much of the time. Their focus is on themselves, and they don't know how to get their needs met much less those of their dependent children.

If you're not sure about your maturity level, mentally run through this list.

Maturity Level for Parent/Child Relationship – Checklist.

- Do you know how to meet your needs?
- Do you know how to meet the child's needs?
- Where is your focus?
- Whose needs come first?

If your focus is on you first and the child next, or the child has to share your focus with you most of the time, please seek professional help in order to understand maturity.

Another element of the Emotional Parenting Kit is the environment in which children are being raised. Is the environment one of love? Characteristics of a loving environment are acceptance, enjoyment, appreciation, mutual respect, encouragement, independence, and feeling safe.

As I write this section the family who comes to my mind is our dear friends, the Partons. This couple is rearing their three children in a loving environment. Their relationship with their children says, "Hey, our precious children, we're here for you. We love you no matter what. Because we love you we will set boundaries and support you to stay within them, and when you cross them, we will guide you back on track. There will be consequences, but they will be just, and the punishment will match the crime. We will love you through the discipline period. We will not withhold our love as punishment. When the correction is complete, we will start fresh with forgiveness and optimism." This is a child-focused loving environment, administered by mature parents.

The opposite of a loving environment is a fear-based environment. Anger, threats, guilt, shame, control, rigidity, and hostility characterize a fear-based environment.

Many children are being reared in fearful environments. A fear-based relationship says, " I am controlling you and the situation because you are afraid of me. You are afraid that I will make you feel guilty, yell at you, say cruel things, slap you, beat you, or even kick you out of my house—or my life—in an attempt to make you do what I want you to do."

Fear-based relationships also dismiss or discount the children. In fearful relationships there is emotional abuse or neglect. Sometimes the parent is not emotionally available. The message to the children is, "I provide food, clothing, and shelter, but don't push me for more because I am not capable of giving more than basic physical care." The parent who is using fear as the foundation for the relationship is usually angry and can move to rage very quickly. Being part of the rage cycle is very traumatic for any child.

Fear-based relationships may look like they are working with a few kids. With some children fear can only work a little while, and then they rebel. They fight back physically or mentally, or they physically check out. Either way the relationship is painful. Fear-based relationships can only appear to work so long. The reality is that fear-based relations are not working at all—they destroy the relationship and the children.

Fear environments cause children to struggle in growing emotionally healthy. Some children never overcome their environment of fear and are not emotionally healthy adults.

Different Personalities React Differently to Fear-based Environments

Personality Type	Description of Personality	What Fear Does to These Children	Reaction to a Fear-based Relationship
Promoter Children	These are warm-hearted children. They know how to love. Love makes their world go around. Think of a friendly dog, lapping your face and wagging around your ankles. This is the way yellow group children feel inside. They are lovers of people and life.	Emotionally based. These children are lighthearted and free spirited. Fear imprisons, binds, and twists, these exuberant, expressive children. The old expression, "tied in knots," is an apt description of what fear does to the yellow group children. The knots scar and impair their emotional growth.	Rebels inwardly or outwardly They will either shrink inward or explode. Shrinking looks like unnaturally subdued, depressed and apathetic. Explosion looks like lying and telling you what they think you want to hear. A range of behaviors from obnoxious to rebellious. The rebellion says,"I'm fighting back at the fear, and I will do whatever I can to get outside your controlling boundaries and shock and defy you."

Personality Type	Description of Personality	What Fear Does to These Children	Reaction to a Fear-based Relationship
Planner Children	These are children who like life to be predictable. They want rules and things to be equitable. They have a strong sense of fairness and justice.	Practical and analytical problem-solvers. Fear-based relationships are volatile and are like walking on eggs. One can never predict what is going to happen. This environment destroys these children's sense of order. It takes them off-balance and makes them operate in a manner that violates everything they want and need. Order, justice, and doing relationships the right way are what these children want.	These children in this blue group will absorb much of the guilt and try to be more perfect than ever.

Personality Type	Description of Personality	What Fear Does to These Children	Reaction to a Fear-based Relationship
Producer Children	These are children who like to control their world. They have a strong sense of what is just. They know how it "should be." They have an innate sense of things that are not just. Parents who reign with fear are not just or fair. When this group grows up they will be part of the system that is trying to right the wrongs of society.	Intuitive and logic based. Fear-based environments violate these children's sense of justice. These action-oriented children will try to do something to right the wrong.	I won't get mad, I'll get even, I'll show you! You think I'm bad, I'll give you bad! I'll fight you back. I won't take this sitting down. These children are usually powerful, determined, and driven enough to carry this relationship dysfunction to a level for which the parent is not prepared.

Personality Type	Description of Personality	What Fear Does to These Children	Reaction to a Fear-based Relationship
Peacekeeper Children	These children are tender-hearted. They are kind and caring. Desire for peace is the driving force behind these children. A world that is surrounded in peace, harmony, and balance is a world in which they thrive.	Practical and emotionally based. These green group children are innately kind and gentle. Fear-based environment violates their very core. These balance needing, harmony-seeking children are totally in a world that destroys who they are.	Try to make peace. Cover-up or deny. Withdraw and hide. Most of the children in this group given the choice between fight or flight will choose flight. These are peace-keepers, not fighters. Duck and take cover, stay out of the way. To become invisible is the method these children use to deal with a fear-based home. These children can be passive resistive and have a silent will of iron. So if they ever switch from flight to fight, look out—it will be a major battle.

The Bible tells us that love covers a multitude of sins. Love also conquers and heals much especially in relationships. Love creates an environment that encourages children to grow emotionally healthy and develop into their full potential. Love empowers children to be all that God intended them to be.

Rechecking the contents of the Parenting Kit for Emotional Needs, we find mature people doing the parenting. The parents and children have a loving environment as the foundation for the relationships. These parents have maturity, strong character qualities, plus patience, wisdom, and humor. Unlike the Kit for physical needs the hospital sends home for the first few days, this kit will last a lifetime.

CHAPTER 12

Docotor Foster's Lessons

T his chapter will be a guide for some and a reminder for others. The concepts in this chapter when applied to the lives of children will help them grow toward the people God intended them to be. As adults guiding children we all make mistakes. It is my hope that with this chapter you can review some things you are doing. If change is needed, you can start to implement improvements for the sake of the children.

Dr. Foster was a crusty old pediatrician who was blunt and plain-spoken. On my first visit he said, "I hope you're not going to screw up this kid."

I replied, " I'd like not to." After this first exchange, I was pretty intimated by him. He was past retirement. I came to him when he was busy writing, lecturing, and trying to close his practice. He was only seeing my ten-month-old son because my girlfriend Maureen, who was his neighbor, convinced him he must.

I didn't want to be kicked out before he examined my continually sick child. But I asked the question anyway, "Do you give lessons in 'How Not to Screw Up Your Children?'"

What I didn't know at the time was that I didn't need to ask that question. Because at each future visit he was going to give me a lesson. Dr. Foster was wonderful at helping physically ill children get well. But I believe his true passion was giving parents the lessons. Matt was sick constantly for the first two years of his life, so I got lots of lessons.

That first visit he said, "I see the good, the bad, and the ugly when it comes to parenting.

The parents give me the subjects for my lessons. Today I'm pushing the lesson I call "Stingy with Praise." Fortunately, he went on so I didn't have to ask for more details. "These parents expect miracles out of their kids. Parents forget about things like developmental stages and maturation. You can't push a child to do or behave in a way he or she isn't ready for yet. Yesterday, I saw a twenty-eight month old whose mother has done serious brain damage to the child. According to the police report she was standing outside violently shaking the child and screaming, "Quit acting like a two year old."

As I was absorbing the shock of this story, he went on, "This was an extreme case of unrealistic expectations and a very unhealthy mother. But often I see parents with too high expectations withholding praise for their children's small achievements. They are waiting for the children to do something spectacular. Children's lives are made up of a series of tiny successes. A child gets there when he gets there. But he needs praise every inch along the way. *Don't hold back on praise, it's the food of healthy emotional growth."*

Each visit I anticipated the "How Not to Screw Up Your Kid" lesson. He admitted he'd get a theme and run with it for a few days. Then he'd see another parent do something bad or ugly and champion another lesson for a while. Then he'd move on to a new lesson.

I certainly wish I had recorded all of Dr. Foster's lessons. I didn't. My memory only recalls some. I remember the "Catch Your Child Doing Something Right" lesson. I used that lesson for both my boys. It always brought joy and a sense of well being to both of us when I praised them for doing something right when they thought no one was watching. I took this lesson one step further. At night I would tell their father the "right thing" I'd caught them doing. That way they got positive feedback twice.

Dr. Foster wasn't eloquent—actually he was crude. The "Don't Label Your Kids" lesson was short and to the point. "If you must call your kid a name, call him a jack-ass. He can look in the mirror and decide you are wrong—no four legs, no long tail, and no pointy ears. But don't call him an idiot, moron, or dumbhead because he won't know exactly what an idiot, dumbhead, or moron is. Since you called him one, he believes you. He thinks because you are the adult, you're probably right. So he takes on the label and starts to grow into it!"

In an attempt to recall all the topics of Dr. Foster's lessons for this book, I have become a "parent watcher." There is a park with a playground near my house. One day as I was writing this book, I hit a dry spell. I charged out of my office and headed for the park.

After twenty minutes of observation I remembered another Dr. Foster lesson. I called it the "Broken Record Syndrome." There were five parents in the park, four of them had Broken Record Syndrome. Taylor's mother had a pretty bad case. "Taylor, don't throw sand. Taylor, don't throw sand. Taylor James, do not throw sand. Young man, if you throw sand again, we are going home!" They were still in the park when I left. Taylor was still throwing sand, and his mother was still sounding like a broken record stuck in one place.

Nathan's mother nagged relentlessly about not running in front of the swing.

Kayley's Dad's record was stuck on "staying off the high slide," but Morgan's Mother was the worst. Her body language was tense and rigid, and her voice was shrill. "Morgan, don't fall. Morgan, be careful. Morgan, don't fall. Morgan, don't fall. Morgan, you are going to fall." The only reason this chant stopped was, of course, Morgan fell. I'm happy to report that Morgan was not hurt, and the chant changed to "Morgan, you are going to fall again." I left before her mother's self-fulfilling prophecy came true.

Now what about the fifth parent? This was an older mommy. The first time her child pushed another child she got up brought the child back to the blanket without saying a word. The child sat there protesting loudly for a while. She let a short time lapse after the protesting stopped. She then whispered something in his ear, and he went back to the group. About ten minutes later, he pushed again. The mother got up, folded her blanket, walked over, and took the child by the hand, and they left the park with the mother totally stoic and the child compliantly marching along beside her.

I would love to tell you that I learned Dr. Foster's lesson and raised my children without repetitious nagging that sounded like a broken record. The honesty of our older son, however, convicted me to the contrary.

When our boys were nine and six my husband enrolled them in the YMCA Indian Guides Program. For days afterward they were trying out different Indian names. One night each of them was some sort of bear—Running Bear, Strong Bear etc. Then it was wolves, deer, and eagles. Finally, it was Indian Guides night, and my sons and husband came home sporting headbands with their names. My husband's headband said Big Brave, and the boys were Strong Brave and Running Brave.

They were laughing and snickering as Matt, our Producer nine year old, said, "Hey, Mom, we didn't want you to feel left out so we gave you a name. I quickly envisioned my headband with Shining Star or Courageous Princess written on it. "Well, thank you, what is it?" I asked expectantly. More laughing broke out as Matt stated with authority, "It's Beat 'Em Dead Horse!" I guess my case of Broken Record Syndrome was more severe than I realized.

Recently I spent another session in the park. I hurried home to put this next lesson on paper. Parents, grandparents, and caregivers were out in force at the playground on that day and, believe me, the art of "threatening" is alive and well and living in our parks. The number one threat of the day was, "If you don't stop behavior X, I'll take you home." Two children actually shaped up upon hearing the threat. Several gave it a rest for a while, but were soon up to their old behaviors. Most did not stop, and they also did not go home. Generally, the parents gave up threatening before the child gave up the undesirable behavior.

There was one grandfather who earned Honorable Mention from me. The first time I observed this family weeks ago, his two older grandchildren were out of control. They terrorized every child in the park while grandpa threatened with every threat in the book. Somehow between that first observation and today, this grandfather had figured it out.

As he and the three children arrived, he had a talk with each. The four year old was reminded of a few basic playground safety issues. The two older ones, somewhere in the eight to ten range, were reminded not to fight and bicker with one another and not to pick on anyone—especially their younger sibling. This is when he really got my attention. Before he let them go, he said, "If these rules are not followed, what will happen?" The boys responded with, "We go home and no TV." He then gave each boy a high five and a quick pat on the head that signaled "I love you" and "I know you can do it." When I left, the three brothers were playing together like model children.

Threats have a range from harmless to the ones that, if carried out, would land us in jail. "I'm going to kill you," being the most serious. Occasionally I lost it and became Threat Queen. However, I tried not to become so out of control that I had to use the "Go to Jail" threats. But when I lost it, it wasn't something I felt pleased about later.

To me, the phrase "family vacation" was an oxymoron. What part of taking your small children away from their familiar surroundings, toys, and friends and seat-belting them into a car, driving for hours, and staying in a small room together is a vacation? I was a full-time, stay-at-home Mom. My idea of a vacation was anywhere the children were not!

My husband traveled a great deal and loved the idea of spending two weeks with his boys in some rustic place to enjoy nature. Well, one particular year, the cabin was beyond rustic; it was old, dirty, and small. Nature hikes were not an option because it poured with thunder and lightening for the first five days. In the late afternoon of day five, I knew I was losing it. If I played one more game of "Go Fish," I would do something extreme and probably harmful to one of us. I stood up and announced, "I'm driving into town and eating dinner at the nicest restaurant I can find." I was planning on this being a quiet dinner for one—me. My husband says, "Great idea, boys, let's go." The boys poked, bickered, and complained all the way to town.

The nicest restaurant in town was a mom and pop diner. The boys were still poking and bickering as we were seated. The dinner had disaster written all over it. At that moment, I truly did not like either of my children.

I grabbed, Matt, our older child and hauled him outside. My body language and voice made it very clear that Mommy was not a happy camper. With both my hands grasping Matt's upper arm I said, "This is your only warning. If you are not a perfect child at dinner, I will bring you back out here and rip your arm from your shoulder and then I will beat you over the head with your own arm." He believed me. I returned Matt to the table and grabbed five-year-old Tyler. Tyler was our wild child, I didn't soften the message one bit for him. I don't know if he understood the threat, but he was quiet and wide-eyed through out the evening.

Once I calmed down and looked across the table at my two angelic children, I realized how much I loved then. The parent in me who wanted to be the best I could immediately started a mental conversation with the parent who had made those awful threats. I asked myself questions like: What kind of emotional damage did you do? How could you be so out of control?

As a PostScript—I just called my two sons to ask if they remembered the diner threats. Tyler who was five didn't remember anything about the trip except we celebrated his birthday, and we hid the presents in the forest near the cabin. Matt didn't remember my exact words, but he remember Mom being very "aggro!" The good news is he also remembered playing fun games and exploring after the sun came out. In spite of my threat he remember the trip as positive.

Personality Types and the Lessons

1. Stingy with Praise

Children need all the words of praise and encouragement they can get. Whoever said, "Sticks and stones will break your bones but words can never hurt you," has never looked into the eyes of a child who has just been stabbed with cruel words.

In the book *Raising A Responsible CHILD: Practical Steps to Successful Family Relationship,* by Dr. Don Dinkmeyer and Dr. Gary D. McKay, they talk about a parent's role in formation of who the child becomes. Referring to the parents they state:

> Their dialogue often directly affects the child's self-concept. Phrases that are negative and nagging, that point out faults, tend to build feelings of inadequacy or resistance. Words that focus on assets, that are positive and encouraging, tend to build self-respect and self-esteem. The parents' real success and joy comes from seeing the child emerge as an autonomous and independent individual who is at the same time secure enough to be responsibly interdependent with his parents and society. No job well done is ever easy. Being a parent must be worked at and rewards will follow.

As adults we must set boundaries and guide children. But we must also continually be on the lookout for situations where our words can build up rather than tear down. Seeing children grow stronger in what they positively believe about themselves, because of affirming words, is a huge reward.

Let's talk about praise. Dr. James Dobson in his book, *Hide and Seek,* stated, "It is helpful to distinguish between the concept of *flattery* vs. *praise.* Flattery is unearned. It is what Grandma says when she comes for a visit: "Oh, look at my beautiful little girl! You're getting prettier each day, I'll bet you'll have to beat the boys off with a club when you get to be a teenager!" Or, "My what a smart boy you are." Flattery occurs when you heap compliments upon the child for something he did not achieve.

Praise, on the other hand, is used to reinforce positive, constructive behavior. It should be highly specific rather than general. "You've been a good boy . . ." is unsatisfactory. "I like the way you kept your room straight today" is better. Parents should always watch for opportunities to offer genuine, well-deserved praise to their children while avoiding empty flattery."

Honest, sincere evaluation of what positive things you see the child becoming or doing is the foundation of praise. Dorothy Corkille Briggs in her book, *Your Child's Self Esteem,* stated, "The single most important ingredient in a nurturing relationship is honesty."

Adult Personality Types and the Stingy with Praise Lesson

PROMOTERS	PLANNERS
Encouragers at heart. Positive words taste good in your mouth. You are usually very good at seeing the up side and expressing it. Watch out for flattery that is insincere, over-stated, and fawning. Children sense when praise is sincere and earned.	In your desire to have everyone do things the right or correct way, you can be critical and hard to please. Tell them what they are doing right—not wrong. Most children know when they have done it wrong, but they need reassurance about the right part. Don't hold back your praise until children do it right. Encourage every step of the way. With your praise children have a much better chance of getting it right. Planners usually are good at specific and detailed praise. Just remember to praise step by step.

continued

PRODUCERS	PEACEKEEPERS
Some of you can be very stingy with praise. You hold back the praise until the final product is complete. Do not wait until the result is achieved. Praise the process – each tiny accomplishment. If you hold back the praise, waiting for completion, you may never see completion. Remember it is *process not product* that moves a child toward good self-image. Producers, don't forget to praise your child for character qualities. Acts of kindness, honesty, and becoming a quality person are more important than many accomplishments. Raising a fine human being is much more important than raising a star "human doing."	Champions of children, you are usually good at praise. You understand the building concept of praise and positive affirmations. Be careful not to use too much flattery and move into insincerity. To the silent observers in this green group: don't be silent when it comes to praising and affirming children. Speak up!

2. Catch a Child Doing Something Right

A child's life seems to be a series of "no, don't, or why did you do that?" This lesson is the opposite of those negatives. Catching your children doing something right and complimenting them for it encourages them to want to repeat this positive action again.

Adults must give children rules and guidelines. The "do's" of life. Often when they are doing what we've requested, we don't notice, or we do notice but don't give positive feedback. This Dr. Foster lesson helps us to be proactive, positive, and puts delight and love into a child's world.

Adult Personality Types and the
"Catch a Child Doing Something Right" Lesson

PROMOTERS	PLANNERS
This will appeal to your love of the opposite. If you observe your child doing something positive, affirm him or her, the minute the timing is right. This yellow group can get sidetracked and move on too quickly and forget to affirm. Don't forget the child needs this food for healthy emotional growth.	You will notice and you will affirm at the right time. Just don't be too picky. If they did nine things right and kind of messed up number ten please, please, for the sake of the child, talk about the nine positive things. At another, separate time, kindly work on number ten. Don't let your perfectionism get in the way of praise!
PRODUCERS	**PEACEKEEPERS**
Remember you are placing your attention on process. If he or she is beginning to do something right and it's not finished, catch him in the "off to a good start" stage and affirm him. Verbalize words of encouragement that state you know he can go on and you are there for him.	Be observant and watch for positive behaviors for which you can affirm your child. Peacekeepers are naturally good at affirmations when they are paying attention—so be sure to pay attention.

3. Don't Label Your Kids

Here I would like to add—don't compare one child to another child. By now you have read all about the personality types. You know that even if you have two children with the same personality type, they will be different shades of the group color. *No two humans are exactly alike.*

Comparing is hard *not* to do. However, there is no point. You are not comparing sameness at all. You can't compare apples to oranges or one child to another child. There are just too many differences. In comparisons usually one looks more favorable, and one looks less favorable. How is looking less favorable than someone else going to encourage and build up a child?

The purpose of this book is to build up children and help them grow toward the person God intended them to be. Improve their self-concept rather than diminish it.

Labeling gives children identity good or bad.

In every school there are children whose reputation as a problem child precedes them to the next grade. Lonnie was such a child. Even as a new teacher to his school, I'd heard about Lonnie. At six years of age Lonnie had seen daddy murder mommy. He was living with a foster family near our school. Lonnie's name was on my enrollment list.

Two days before school started, as I was preparing my classroom for the new school year, I looked up and saw a hollow-eyed, round shouldered, handsome boy standing in the doorway. I knew instinctively that this was Lonnie. I said, "Hi, I'm Mrs. Barnes, what's your name?

"Lonnie," he stoically responded.

"Well, Lonnie, your name is on my class list. I'm really glad you stopped by. I'm a new teacher here, and your file seems to be lost." The truth was, his written file was missing, but the verbal file was clearly in my mind. Disturbed, disruptive, raging, and emotionally unbalanced were just a few of the words in my mental file.

I took a fresh new file from my drawer and said, " Lonnie, why don't we fill out a new file for you. I'm sure you are the person who knows the most about you." At that moment a sparkle of light came into his lifeless eyes. For the next half an hour Lonnie and I filled out the form. When completed, the profile was of the child I believe Lonnie would have been before his mother was murdered.

I used the labels on Lonnie's new file to guide Lonnie that year. Labels he gave himself. Cooperative, smart, good student, and great kid were some of these labels. Lonnie and I had a wonderful year. He lived up to his labels.

Comparing and negative labeling can cause permanent damage. Not every child gets a chance to rewrite the labels someone else has put on him or her. Be careful not to create such negative label or comparisons.

Adult Personality Types and the Don't Label Your Kids Lesson

PROMOTERS	PLANNERS
You, like all the personality types, have labeled and compared. Because you have such big hearts and are cheerleaders of life you will understand this concept.	You are a very realistic group—no-nonsense and practical. Sometimes giving the benefit of the doubt is hard for you. You call shots as you see them. But don't call children negative names—they might grow into them. Try to look through the eyes of love with the children in your life.
PRODUCERS	**PEACEKEEPERS**
Don't 'bottom line' the children in your life. Practice giving them the benefit of the doubt. Mercy often works over justice and is more productive which I know you can appreciate.	You are the kindest among us. Labels and comparisons are ways to exclude and ostracize. You understand acceptance and inclusion. You know the damage that can be done with labeling and comparing. Don't be guilty of it.

4. Threats vs. Logical Consequences

The rules for using threats are simple. Don't. Threats are warnings that float in the atmosphere. Threats are a loose and ineffective way of trying to communicate what you expect to your children. State the behavior you want the child to model. Then state the consequences if he or she doesn't behave accordingly. As insurance, ask the child to repeat the desired behavior and the consequence. Then, do one of two things. One, relax knowing your child is going to follow your command. Or two, get ready to immediately act upon the consequence.

Note about consequences:

When my children were in grade school, I was part of a group of mothers who would read a different book on child raising each month. At our meetings, we would discuss the concepts in the book and share how we were using them to be more effective as mothers. When we were studying the concept of logical consequences from the book *Children the Challenge* by Dreikurs, one of the mothers shared the following story.

Her son, age eleven, had a history of losing jackets, sweaters, and coats. She said, "I kept threatening, I'm not buying anymore warm things to wear. But he'd lose his last jacket, we'd have a cold spell, and I'd worry about him getting sick, so I'd buy another jacket. Finally, I decided this is the last jacket I'm buying."

She gave the child the new jacket with a note. The note said, "This is the last jacket I am going to buy you. If you want to wear this jacket, you must sign below that you believe this is a promise not a threat."

He signed the note, but the mother was sure the son really didn't think she'd do it. Two weeks later the jacket was gone. She taped the signed note to the back door so he could see it every day when he left in the cold for school.

She said to our group, "This is really hard I'm worried about him getting a cold, but I think I'm more worried about what people will think of me when they see him walking around in the rain without a jacket."

Another group member said, "I don't know what other people will think but I will think, there goes a child whose mother finally figured out the concept of logical consequences."

Make sure consequences are the natural result of not behaving as requested. As adults we arrange the logical consequence, but the child must experience them as logical in nature.

Adult Personality Types and the Threats Lesson

PROMOTERS	PLANNERS
Your highly verbal group is usually guilty of using threats. You also have a developed imagination, so you can make up some real out of the ordinary threats. Attention yellow group, you don't get extra points for wild and crazy threats. State the behavior you expect and the consequence if not followed and stop talking.	You need to be divided. You have the no nonsense people who don't threaten. You state the rule once and expect it to be followed. When it is not, you take action. Those in the second group use nagging and whining. You have developed such a bad habit, you don't even know you are practically sing-songing the threats. Stop, no one is listening, and you are driving everyone crazy with the noise.
PRODUCERS	**PEACEKEEPERS**
You are often low in the "repeated threat" department. However, sometimes you are high in the "punishment does not match the crime" department. Because you like everything effective and efficient, you become annoyed when children behave like spirited children. Some Producers over react with too strict a punishment for the infraction. Use the concept of logical consequences.	You gentle spirits are not comfortable with the kind of out of control threats I made to my two boys at the diner. You usually don't threaten to break arms or kill as other groups might. Your group's threats sound more like a plea. If threatening is called for and the harmony is gone, you are not happy. You are pleading with the child to shape up so peace can be restored. Try to avoid pleading and clearly state expectations.

5. Broken Record Syndrome

Restating your command over and over makes you look like a talking head and your children seem hearing impaired. State your request once. Then take action immediately when your request is ignored or disregarded. The cure for this syndrome is— stop mouthing and start moving. Physically help the children pick up their toys, move out of the way of harm, or move them away from others.

Adult Personality Types and the Broken Record Syndrome (BRS) Lesson

PROMOTERS	PLANNERS
Your are high verbals. Most of you just generally like to talk. Giving little attention to details, you usually have no idea how many times you've already made a request to the child. Most Promoters have a pretty bad case of BRS. Promoters, say it once, if the child doesn't take action— GET UP and physically help them to action your request.	You tend to nag and worry. But, because of the systems, structure, and order in your lives, most of this group has only a light case of BRS. Planners, state it one time only. Then action the plan. Do not revist it later!
PRODUCERS	**PEACEKEEPERS**
You are action oriented. Repetition and belaboring a point is not something you like to do. It is not effective. You probably do not have BRS.	You are so kind and gentle you want to give the child the benefit of the doubt. Peacekeeper parents, unless your child is hearing impaired, trust that they heard you the first time. Stop repeating it. Most of you have pretty severe cases of BRS. Get a plan of action. Tell your child in advance what the consequences will be. Then stop talking and move into your plan of action.

CHAPTER 13

Speaking Out
for the Kids

Whated I talk to children about what's in this book I ask them, "What else should I talk to parents about?" The number one answer is homework.

Of course, most of them say, "Tell them not to make us do it!"

I smile and say, "You know I'm not going to say that. So, what should I tell them?" This is what I hear from the children.

Help With School Work

Parents trying to help their children with schoolwork is often a potentially difficult area. Homework needs to be completed, and the parents are trying to help. Getting homework finished seems to turn nice families into not so nice families.

The average American family is tense. Job pressure, financial concerns, and demanding schedules create tension. Everything and everybody must move efficiently and effectively if the schedule is going to stay intact.

Most children's efficient and effective button is stuck somewhere between "I don't know how" and "I don't want to." They are just kids being kids, dawdling along, becoming sidetracked, or completely forgetting what they were supposed to do.

Children are not born with this feeling of pressure. We adults bring it on them. How many times have children heard "Hurry up," or "Now it's your fault we are late" or "Hurry with your homework. I do not have all night to help you." These are pressure statements that put tension into kids' lives.

Trying to help your children do better in school is often a source of tension even in a relaxed home. The odds are stacked against both the parents and the children. Usually it's the end of the day, and time is running out. Everyone is tired. Trying to work with your children is often a no win situation.

The potential for disaster here is huge. There are many reasons why helping with homework isn't successful. Here are a few of the biggest offenders:

- The parent wasn't at school and often doesn't have the communication correct.
- Parents don't explain it like the teacher does.
- Parents are pushing their personality types on the children.
- Parents are pushing their study methods on the students.
- Children want to play or watch TV rather than do school work.
- Everyone is tired.
- The track record on this whole homework experience has been negative. Neither parents nor children went into this time with positive attitudes.

This scene can be a breeding ground for frustration, anger, cruel words, hurt feelings, and tears. For most families trying to help children improve in school ranges from a generally unsettling experience to a nightmare. The parents nag and threaten while the children actively rebel or go passive resistive, saying they will do it but knowing they won't.

Suggestions for Working with the Personality Types of Your Children

The Promoter children will want to do homework when the mood strikes, which may be never. They will want to do it in a non-conventional place and usually with music or other distractions. Even for Promoter parents dealing with these children, the homework situation might be a challenge.

Let Promoter children have some choices and the parents have some choices. A suggestion is that the parents chose the time, and the children chose the place. Let them have low music if they insist—but if the grades go down, the music goes off. Give them as many options as you can to structure their own homework setting. If the floor works, let them stay there. Give them several opportunities for breaks or sidetracking. They are easily sidetracked so build it into the homework time. I call these "jump ups." They can "jump up" and get a snack or whatever distraction they think they *must* do. Give them X amount of "jump ups" per homework session with a time limit on each "jump up." The children then get the freedom to choose how and when to use the "jump ups." Tear up strips of paper and number them so you can keep track. Yes, some of these children might try to fool you about how many "jump ups" they have left.

Note to Planner, Producer, Peacekeeper, and maybe even Promoter parents: these children may handle distraction better than you think they can. Keep extra school supplies hidden away for emergencies.

These children are going to take constant adjusting like driving a car on bumps and curves. Helping with homework with the Promoter children will not be a cruise control situation. You must be informed. Communicate constantly with the school to know what the assignments are and when they are due. Promoter children are infamous for what I call "Late Dropping."

It's Thursday night at nine o'clock, and they drop out the fact that they just remembered the three-page report that was assigned a week ago, which is due in the morning. They are going to start it now. But first they are out of the kind of paper the teacher said it had to be on and could you go to the store for paper.

I told you, Promoter children involve a bumpy ride and constant adjustment. Being informed, giving options, and offering choices will make for a smoother ride. Also in this situation there is the logical consequence option. The child may have to go to bed, receive an F, and next time start the assignment in a timely manner.

Most parents report that Planner children usually do their homework without much prodding. Let them decide where to work and how. You might need to give some input on when. The problem with these children is perfection in all things. Planner children dissolve into tears because the paper is too messy or the report isn't the perfect way they planned it in their head. Help these children lighten up on themselves. They tend to be all or nothing thinkers. It is a perfect paper or a horrible paper. Help them find the middle ground.

Producer children, if they are competitive and have decided to win at this school challenge, will manage themselves. Most of these children can handle a great deal of independence. They are self-starters. The problem with these children comes when the adult tries to interfere and tell them what and how to do it. Then you have a fight for control. Sometimes to get control, the children may stop doing the homework. Watch them. If they are handling the homework situation, then leave them alone.

What about Producer children who don't want to win at the grade game? Find out what they do want to achieve or accomplish. Help them realize they can get to whatever it is they want to achieve after the homework is finished. Once you show this pragmatic child that homework will be first, they usually do it so they can move on to what it is they want. Here again, parents, try to give them as much freedom as you possibly can. You don't want to fight over control. As adults we might decide the one or two big things and let them have all the little decisions.

Peacekeeper children like your help. Guard against doing too much for them. Some like you to sit with them while others are satisfied to know you are available to answer questions. These children are collaborative and like working with others. Like the Promoter children, communicate with teachers so you know the homework assignments. If it is a big project that is coming due, start as soon as you can. Most green group children do not like the last minute rush. Help these children plan out the work piece by piece. Help them do their homework at a steady pace that is comfortable for them. Guard against these children procrastinating then becoming overwhelmed. If they fall to pieces it is difficult to get them glued back together to get the homework done. They can function in a cluttered environment and might even prefer it. If they can learn in a messy space, ignore it.

Helping Your Child and Having Fun

Some of the largest audiences I've spoken to are educators, many of whom are also parents. Even in this circle I discovered that helping their own children at home is often a problem. My topics are usually about meeting the needs of the children in the classroom by increased understanding of who they are—their personality types. But in every question and answer session I always get some questions about homework.

Several years ago, after my speech to teachers, I had a question and answer session. The topic of the first question was homework. The audience gave a collective groan. I was so surprised at the negative response, I asked, "Do even teachers who are parents have trouble with the homework situations?" The audience all started talking at once, to me, to their neighbors, and to themselves. For the rest of the day I was bombarded with homework nightmare stories from teacher/parents.

Finally I heard a wonderful success story. Allan Jarviss was a principal who stopped me in the hall. He said, "I was at both of your speeches today. I wear the red Producer shirt first and the yellow Promoter shirt immediately over the top. Does that make me an orange group person?"

He went on without giving me a chance to answer. "I solved the homework hassle with my kids years ago, and here's how—with games."

"What kinds of games?" I questioned.

"Well, as a principal I had access to some games that were fun and educational," he said. "I started playing educational games with my kindergarten son because he didn't have any homework and felt left out because the other two were getting so much attention. I might add that the attention the other two were getting was more negative than positive. I hated helping with homework, but my kids were in my school. They had to do their homework! Once I started playing games with my six year old the other two suddenly got their homework done in record time so they could play, too."

"Then they started coming home from school getting their homework done without my help or nagging so we could use homework time for games. I can tell you, I started to look forward to homework time and so did the kids. Plus, because we were playing educational games the kids learned new things. Now, I'm a grandfather, and one night a week I go over to my daughter's house for homework or game night. I taught my five-year-old grandson to read with a game called *Jr. Phonics.*™"

Parents, if homework time is unpleasant, stop, take a new approach. Use the Allan Jarviss method. Try to rewrite history. Instead of the usual homework war tonight change the whole scenario. Use the homework time to play an educational game. If helping them with homework has been an unpleasant experience without much success, then change the atmosphere. Yelling and screaming hasn't worked, so try relaxation and laughter. They may flunk the spelling test, but hey, you are changing a cycle that has been negative and hasn't worked anyway.

For you Planner parents I know you are having trouble with this idea. Number one, it's change. Two, it sounds irresponsible. And three, it's just too radical. But I bet that if you review your track record on this homework help situation you'll find that it could use some levity. The tension is doing some real damage to your family. Be spontaneous and try something new! It will be good for all of you. Let your children see you in the light of a playmate for thirty minutes. It will not undermine your authority.

Producers, I know you are saying, "You've got to be kidding. Let them off the hook for homework for one night?" Yes, that what I'm suggesting, and here's why it's effective and efficient. The situation has become negative and counter productive so you've got to do something to reverse this trend.

Start slowly, pick one night a week for game time. Once you get this new plan in operation, the kids might hurry with their homework so they have more game time. Educational games are your answer. There is hope, particularly if your children are having math or reading problems. The game teaches the skills or concepts, and all you have to do is play and enjoy your children. This will be a win/win situation. Educational games do all the *work* you have the *fun*.

Playing games reverses the tension. The game setting is casual. Your children just participate and don't have to produce anything. There is no pressure on anyone. Parents are relaxed. The children see this lighter side, and they relax.

The benefits of playing games with your children:

1. Creating Positive Memories

My husband and I volunteer one week a year at a summer camp for children who are in the foster care system. The campers come from backgrounds of abuse, neglect, or abandonment and have been removed from their homes and placed in foster homes or group homes. The goal of Royal Family Kids' Camp is to *create positive memories*. One of the campers' favorite evening activities is playing board or card games with their counselors.

Another example involves our friends the Brownlys. Their grown children still talk about Wednesday nights growing up. This was the night when they had silly dinner and games. Silly dinner consisted of finger food like vegetables and dip, crackers, cheese, and fruit for dessert. The food was on paper plates on the counter top, and they could snack and play games. They recall that Mom was relaxed and dishes were non-existent. The positive memories are of their family laughing, teasing, and having fun together.

2. Seeing the Family in the Best Light

Twelve-year-old Jonathan said, "I like playing games because my dad decompresses, hangs with us, and is actually a cool guy."

Nine-year-old Hailey said, "Playing games with the family is my favorite thing. This is the only time I see my parents laugh."

In another family, Pat, mother of four said, "Stopping my crazy schedule, forcing myself to sit down and play games with my children reminded me that I have bright delightful children."

Another example was Barbara and Ed who said, "We were forced to play games because it rained every day of our vacation. We had so much fun, laughing with and at each other, our kids were sad to see the vacation come to an end. We promised an hour of games once a week, and we have kept the promise. We found games are a great way to bring the family together."

3. Experiencing Life vs. Watching Life

According to the A.C. Neilsen Company, the average child spends 38.5 minutes in meaningful conversation with their parents per week. The average child watches television 1,680 minutes a week. In this hi-tech world our children are gazing into a screen much of their lives. This screen gazing is solitary and inactive. It encourages isolation and disconnection. Playing games is about interaction, communicating, and bonding. Our children will be taking an active part in a live family event instead of passively sitting and watching pretend TV families live life.

4. Old Fashion Good Time

There are reasons that some things stand the test of time, and game playing is one of them. With most games anyone can win. With the element of luck, wild cards, and rolls of the dice, it's a level playing field. A person who is smaller, less educated, in other words the child, can win. What great fun to beat an adult at a game.

I have a young friend name Tony who is nine years old. One rainy day we were playing *The Phonics Game*™. I know how to read, and he struggles with reading, but he beat me seven games in a row. Every time I see Tony his face lights up and he says, "Remember the time I beat you seven games in a row." For a child to claim victory over an adult is just an old fashioned, good time.

5. Everyone Wins

Being an educator I have seen the positive effects of educational games. You can help your children while having a good time. Parents are constantly sharing their frustration about not knowing how to help their children do better in school. One overwhelmed Mom said, "I know I should work with my kids at home, but all we do is fight and argue."

Play educational games and laugh and learn. Games help parents enjoy their children, and games help children remember that Mom and Dad are fun.

My husband and I are involved with giving our time and our hearts to foster children. Many of these children struggle academically and are behind in basic reading and math skills. We got *The Phonics Game*™, Jr. *Phonics*™, and *The Math Game*™ to play with them.

We find with games, we can quickly assess what the children know and what they need to learn. While using the game and having fun, it doesn't seem like we're assessing where the children are in their skill levels—but we are. The games build level upon level so we keep playing until they say, "I got it!" Then we move to the next level and the next new skill. We are helping these children learn basic math and reading skills, and they feel good about themselves at the same time. As I observe these children I can practically see new self-confidence growing in them. Some are succeeding at reading and math for the first time, thanks to these games.

Playing games promotes family harmony, bonding, and love! With educational games you can also help children learn better skills and increase self-confidence. Everybody wins.

Have Some Fun With This Story

The Emperor's New Clothing
One Story – Four Different Children
and their Personality Types

Suggestion for Parents: *Tell your children the old version of the story The Emperor's New Clothing. Then read this new version of the story with your children. When you are finished ask each child which child's reaction is the most like the reaction he or she would have if watching the parade.* **Listen** *as each child answers. This could be an opportunity for insight for you and some open dialogue with your children.*

Ten-year-old Henry had an excellent view of the parade. He planned ahead and brought a stool upon which to stand. For weeks Henry and the people of the kingdom had waited to see the Emperor's new clothing. The moment he laid eye on the Emperor, Henry's internal voice said, "There is a problem. This is a big problem. The Emperor isn't wearing new clothing. The Emperor isn't wearing any clothing. The Emperor is marching down the street completely nude, believing he's wearing new clothes made with invisible micro fibers. This isn't right. The problem must be solved."

His analytical mind whirled. Let's review the data. How could the experts let this happen? Are the experts really experts? Where did this new clothing project break down? This was supposed to be the latest technology in invisible micro fiber fabric. But from another part of Planner Henry's brain entered the voice that plagues Planners and sends them into analysis paralysis. "Maybe I'm the problem. I'm just a kid and not sophisticated enough to see such high tech clothing. If only I knew more about fabrics, clothing construction, and tailoring, then I could solve this problem, if it is a problem at all. Is there a problem or is it just me?"

At that moment he spotted his friend Joseph across the street and down the way. Now Joseph was someone who had an opinion on everything. He had a powerful way of convincing others and making things happen. Henry decided to watch Joseph and see his reaction.

Joseph also had an excellent view of the parade. He was, in fact, seated on the edge of the official viewing stand. Before the parade had began Producer Joseph stationed himself on the stand with a clipboard and some official looking badges. Even though he was just a kid, no one questioned him because his demeanor said, "I'm an important part of this event. Don't mess with me."

The minute Joseph saw the Emperor he had to squelch a giant roar of laughter bursting to escape his mouth. He kept his face perfectly straight so as not to betray the racing thoughts darting through his mind. He mused, "Well, my, my, my, someone has conned the Emperor big time. I can't believe that someone who has risen to the status of Emperor could fall for this. The Emperor is looking like a complete incompetent! The guy deserves to walk down the street naked for being such a fool. Far be it from me to blow his cover, or should I say his uncover!"

Little Katherine was holding her breath with excitement. It seemed like she'd been standing here waiting for hours looking at nothing but the backs of tall adults. But now, leaning down she had found a slice of a view between a thin ladies legs. Finally there was the Emperor right in front of her. Katherine's breath spilled out in a gasp. The Emperor wasn't wearing any clothing. She was immediately sad for the Emperor and overwhelmed about what to do. Peacekeeper Katherine didn't want to upset anyone. She rationalized, "Maybe I'm the only one who noticed. If no one else noticed, then the parade would go on. The celebration would continue, people would be happy, and the Emperor wouldn't be embarrassed. I'm definitely not telling what I think."

Rebecca rushed to the end of the parade route. Late as usual she hoped she hadn't missed getting to see the Emperor all decked out in his fancy new clothes. Looking at all the people she wondered how she would ever see. But life had a way of dealing favorably with Promoting Rebecca. Just as she arrived on the scene, she spied her very tall uncle who said, "How would you like to sit on my shoulders so you can see?"

Sitting high above the crowd Rebecca saw the Emperor prancing down the street. Her first thought came immediately out of her mouth. "The Emperor isn't wearing any clothing," she shrieked in disbelief.

Her uncle said, "Out of the mouths of babes..."

I encourage you to explore with your children who are old enough the concept of their personality types. Be sure to focus on the positive strengths and use what you have learned about the blind spots to guide them more effectively.

Children who have been introduced to their personality types gain a greater sense of self worth. My Promoter friend Johanna used the four personality types concept with her Sunday school class. One little Peacekeeper child said, "If God made me a Peacekeeper, then I want to be the best me I can be."

Thank You Notes

From the KIDS

Dear Grown-ups,

Hi, My name is Jake, and I'm a Producer. A bunch of us kids wanted to thank you for reading the book and trying to be adults who raise us the right way. The other kids were just standing around talking about it. Enough talking! So while they are still figuring it out, I'm going to write my part and be done with it!

Thanks a lot. I know I'm just a kid, and I don't know everything yet, but I'm working on it. But I know I really hate it when the adults in my life don't know what they are doing.

My Mom says, "Heaven help the teachers and coaches I get who are weak or incompetent."

I know what incompetent means because my Mom explained it. I was surprised that grown-ups could be incompetent seeing as how they are so old, but some really are incompetent. I sure hope those adults read this book. Maybe it will help them to shape up and get smart.

I need the adults in my life to be shaped up because sometimes I just go right up and tell them they are wrong. My Dad called it something like challenging authority, whatever that is.

I want to be President of the United States when I grow up. I don't need some adult making a mistake with my future. That's why I'm glad about the book. Now everyone will know how to help me. None of my friends want to be President. My friend, Logan, wants to own a shop that fixes cars like his Dad does. Jeremy wants to be a policeman like his brother. They don't think I can be President, but I think I can.

Thank you for reading *The KID Book* and trying to be a competent grown-up.

Jake

Now I'll find someone else to write to you.

Dear Adults,

Well, that pushy Producer says someone has to go next, so I will. I'm a Planner. My name is Adam. I sure liked the part in the book where it explains about how much blue group kids like to try to do things the very best we can. Sometimes, people just tell me to hurry up and finish when I don't even have it right. I also liked the part where it said we are usually good kids in school. I really try, but it seems like sometimes other kids try to get me in trouble. I really don't like to be in trouble. I like to follow the rules, and I think everyone should. Sometimes kids tease me. They say I'm a goodie, goodie. But I'm not. I just don't want to make a bunch of mistakes and get into trouble.

My mom is always late to stuff, and I hate to be late. I showed her the part that says kids like me hate to be late.

My mom never has to tell me to clean my room. I can't stand messy things. I have to share a bathroom with my two sisters. They leave hair junk everywhere, and the floor is always sticky with hairspray. They are both very messy. Their room is like a junk pile. When I grow up I'm not going to let my kids be messy.

Thank you for reading the book and trying to do the best you can.

Well, that's my part, I hope I did it right.

> Sincerely Yours,
> Adam

Dear Big People,

My name is Katelin, and I guess I'm a Peacekeeper because I do like peace. I know I hate it when people yell and are mean to each other. I try real hard not to make people mad at me. I stay real quiet so I don't get them mad. If big people read the book and find out how much it hurts us green group kids when they are being angry and crazy maybe they will stop. I hope they stop.

I like the part about not rushing us kids. My parents are always telling me to hurry up with getting ready and to jump in the car, cause we are late every morning. Sometimes the ride to school makes me sick in my stomach because everyone is so tight like robots, and they don't talk calm. Why do they always have to be so nervous?

I like my teacher this year. She isn't mean like Mrs. Martin last year was. She understands me, and she talks to just me sometimes. We talk about cats. We both love cats.

Thank you for reading the book. I don't know what else to say.

> Your Friend,
> Katelin

Hello Folks,

Hi, I'm Alexis, but I like to be called Allie. I'm in the fourth grade. I have long blond hair, and everyone says I'm going to grow up to be a model. I would love to be a model. It would be so fun to wear all those pretty clothes and have people fix my hair in the latest styles and wear all that make-up. I think traveling to all the places models go to have their pictures taken would be really great.

One of my best friends, Molly, says wanting to be a model is a dumb idea because every girl wants to be a model, and there wouldn't be enough jobs for everyone. Molly wants to be a veterinarian. I wouldn't want to touch all those sick animals. She said I had to get a second choice so I decided I want to be a television news reporter. I'd like to be the one who goes out to the place that's having the fire and talk about what's going on.

I have two more bests friends, April and Carley. They are my best friends, but I have lots of other friends. I have my school best friends like Molly, April, and Carley. Then I have my neighborhood best friends. They don't all go to my school. So they are just my friends after school, on Saturdays and Sundays, and during the summer. Then on Sundays I have two best friends in Sunday school, Delaney and Marney.

My favorite part of the book was about all those A's for yellow group kids. I like it when I have an audience, and I can put on a show. I like compliments. I try to tell my friends good things about them. I know it makes them feel good. I can tell by the way they smile after I tell them something good. I only say true stuff. I don't make up things about them that are not true. BYE!

Cheers,
Allie

P. S. Thanks for reading the book and understanding us!

A Thank You Note

From the Author

Dear Readers,

I hope you have gained new insight from this book regarding your relationships with the children in your lives. Being a Promoter, I want to hear from you. What information helped you the most? How are you going to use what you've learned? And of course, let me know the success stories — the difference this book is making in your life.

I want to give you the opportunity to respond. Please find an 800 number and a Web site address on the next page. The Web site will also give information about ordering books and personality type assessments for children, as well as providing information on my seminars.

On behalf of the children, thank you for reading **The Kid Book.** And thank you for trying to speak the language of understanding personality types, which children translate as the language of love.

Blessings and Joy,
Vicki L. Barnes

Vicki Barnes Seminars

Guiding People Toward Positive Relationships

If you've enjoyed this book and want to...

- Order additional books
- Determine your children's personality type
- Learn more about Vicki Barnes Seminars

Visit: **www.VB-Seminars.com**

Call: **Vicki Barnes Seminars at 800-965-8008**

Vicki's popular seminar topics include:

- **Understanding the KIDS in Your Life**
  High impact message for parents, teachers, coaches, specialty, or church groups.

- **Team Building or Effective Communication**
  Both are effective for corporate groups, schools, nonprofit groups, church staffs.

- **Customer C.A.R.E. – Creating A Repeat Environment**
  For any organization, corporation or company with customer contact.

- **Stress Management**
  Any group or organization dealing with the complexities of working with people.

- **Entrepreneurial Exploration Workshops**
  Especially helpful for those considering launching a new business.

- **Career Planning and Self Assessment**
  For entering, changing or refocusing a career.

Order Form

Send this form along with payment to:

For Kids Only, Inc.
P. O Box 10237
Newport Beach, CA 92658-0237

Or order from our web site: **www.fko.org**

	Qty	Each	Amount
The KID Book – *Vicki L. Barnes*		$14.95	
50 Red Hot Ideas for Children's Ministry – *Dean Lies*		$11.95	
God's Power on Stage – *Kathleen Chapman:*			
• **How to Start a Dynamic Children's Musical Theater**		$ 9.95	
• **25 Dramas for Junior Kids**		$11.95	
• **25 Dramas for Primary Kids**		$11.95	
• **Holiday Dramas for Kids**		$11.95	
		Sub Total	
	California residents only – add 7.75% Tax		
	(Add $3/book for Shipping & Handling) S/H		
		TOTAL	

Name _____ Date _____

Company _____ E-mail _____

Street Address _____

City/Province _____ State _____

Zip/Postal Code _____ Country _____ Phone _____

☐ **VISA.**   ☐ **MasterCard**   ☐ Check/Money Order *(Payable to For Kids Only, Inc.)*

Card No. ////////////////////////

Exp. date _____ Signature _____